Revise for OCR GCSE Resistant Materials

David Carlson

Heinemann

OCR
RECOGNISING ACHIEVEMENT

Heinemann Educational Publishers
Halley Court, Jordan Hill, Oxford OX2 8EJ
Part of Harcourt Education Limited

Heinemann is a registered trademark of
Harcourt Education Limited

First published 2003
07 06 05 04 03
10 9 8 7 6 5 4 3 2 1

British Library Cataloguing in Publication Data
A catalogue record for this book is available from the British Library on request.

ISBN 0 435 41716 9

Typeset by Tech-Set Ltd
Printed and bound in the UK by Bath Press Limited

Acknowledgements
Every effort has been made to contact copyright holders of material reproduced in this book. Any omissions will be rectified in subsequent printings if notice is given to the publishers.

Tel: 01865 888058 email: info.he@heinemann.co.uk

Contents

How to use this book

This book has been written as a revision guide for students studying the GCSE Design and Technology (D&T): Resistant Materials – OCR specification.

It can be used in conjunction with the following OCR resources:
- GCSE Resistant Materials for OCR – student book
- GCSE OCR Design & Technology: Resistant Materials specification.

The book covers the content and guidance notes included in the specification. It contains a basic breakdown of the information and knowledge required to ensure that you are well prepared to answer any question set on any aspect of the specification content.

For more detailed coverage and information you should refer to the OCR student book as listed above. This deals with the specification content in more detail. You should also keep yourself up to date with current developments within new technologies, processes and materials by visiting a range of resources – from the Internet to the local newspapers.

How this book is set out

This book is clearly set out with the following sections:

Specification reference points

The specification reference points are included in a box at the start of each section. Each section starts with the relevant specification reference link and follows with the content in the same order as the specification (written in easy to understand terms under the heading 'This section will cover:').

Key words

These are designed to help you focus and remember the important words and terms linked to the content covered in each section.

Key points

These are designed to provide a summary of the most important points in the section. These are useful as a quick, recap revision source.

Questions

You can answer the questions at the end of each section using the information contained within the section. As good examination practice you can either:
- use the text when answering the questions, or
- answer the questions without it and use the text to check your understanding.

The answers are at the back of the book.

Activities

The activities at the end of each section have been devised to:
- give you practice in applying the knowledge you have gathered from the section, and
- provide strategies to restructure the information so that it is easy to remember.

Exam guidance

This section summarises the scheme of assessment and question paper requirements outlined by OCR in the specification. It also contains useful tips and guidelines to help you prepare for the written examination.

The GCSE Design and Technology: Resistant Materials examinations allow students to demonstrate their specialist knowledge, skills and understanding of resistant materials through questions on the subject content outlined in the specification.

Question paper requirements

The combination of question papers taken for a GCSE in Resistant Materials for OCR depends upon:

- tier of entry
- full or short course.

Tier of entry

- **Papers 1 and 3** – Foundation tier papers. These allow students to achieve grades G–C. Both these papers are 1 hour 15 minutes long.
- **Papers 2 and 4** – Higher tier papers. These allow the students to achieve grades D–A*. Both these papers are 1 hour 30 minutes long.

Full or short course

- **Full course students** complete **both** question papers from their tier of entry.
- **Short course students** complete only **one** question paper. For example, Paper 1 (Foundation tier) or Paper 2 (Higher tier).

Papers 1 and 2 include a product analysis question based on information contained in the question paper. The focus of the product analysis question will **not** follow that of the published theme for Papers 3 and 4.

Papers 3 and 4 also contain a product analysis question but this is based on a theme published before the examination. The theme can be researched before the examination is taken, but information gathered **cannot** be taken into the examination.

Structure of the examination

There are five compulsory questions on each examination paper and each question is worth 10 marks. The questions are divided into sub-sections. They start off easy, becoming harder towards the end of the paper. (You must give more detail in your answers at the end of the paper and use more technical language.)

Examination technique

On the following page is an example of the type of question found on the examination paper – there are more examples at the back of this book. Read the tips carefully to find out how you can successfully fulfill the requirements of the question.

1 A clothes hook for a child's bedroom is shown in Figure 1.

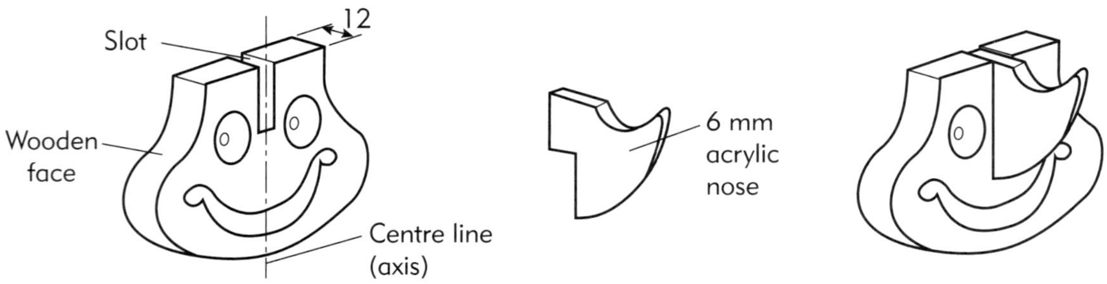

Figure 1

a) One of the areas of research the designer needed to consider was the weight of clothes. State **three** other areas of research the designer would need to consider.

1 ______________________________

2 ______________________________

3 ______________________________

b) The outline of half the face shape has been drawn in Figure 2.

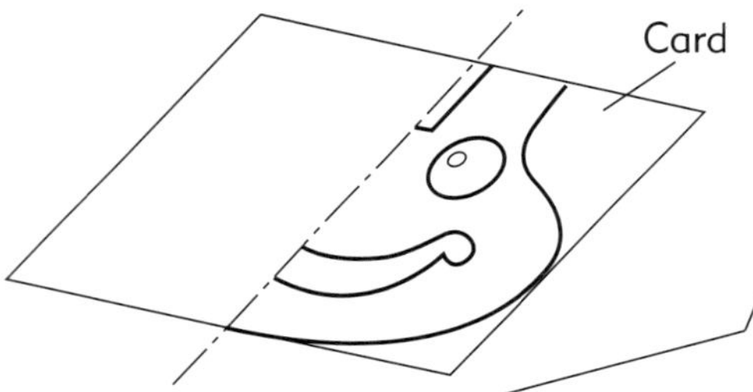

Figure 2

i) Describe how an accurate card template can be made using this information to assist in the manufacture of the face.

____

____

____

ii) When manufacturing a batch of 50 or more identical faces, card is unsuitable for use as a template.
State one reason why card is unsuitable ______
______________________________ (1)

Alternative material ______________________
______________________________ (1)

c) Using notes and sketches, modify the design to show how the parts of the clothes hook could be secured in position without using glue. (3)

Tips

- Time available to answer each question:
  15 minutes for foundation tier
  18 minutes for higher tier.
- Words such as 'list', 'state' or 'name' usually indicate one-word answers are acceptable.
- Words such as 'identify', 'describe' and 'analyse' usually require a more detailed, structured answer.
- The marks allocated for each part of the question are shown in brackets at the end of the question. This is a good guide to the amount of detail needed in the answer, i.e. the 2 marks allocated indicate that two different answers are needed.
- The amount of space (number of lines) provided for the answer is another 'clue' to how detailed the answer should be.
- When answering design type questions, try to use as much of the space available as possible.
- When asked to 'use notes and sketches' try to make your sketches large and clear. Use notes to expand upon the information shown in the sketch.
- If you are asked to design or draw an item, look for the number of marks allocated for it and include at least that number of features in the design. Some indication of colour in design questions will be expected.
- A product analysis question will always ask you to apply your knowledge to the wider effects of design and technology on society and industrial practice alongside your understanding of the design and make process.
- Spelling is not critical, but handwriting is. Marks are not lost if a word is spelt incorrectly but they are if the examiner cannot read the answer!
- Remember to use the knowledge you have gained from your internal assessment (coursework) piece. Questions often refer to the design and make process which you have actively experienced.

Designing and Making

Developing and writing a design brief

This section will cover:

- How design problems are identified.
- Identifying the users and the intended market for the product.
- Developing a design brief for a marketable product.

How design problems are identified

A variety of information sources, such as text, drawings, photographs and newspaper or magazine articles, can be used to identify design problems. Sometimes an information source can be professional advice or market research. Information sources give you a starting point from which products can be designed and made.

Consider the following:

The Design and Technology department at my school has been approached by a local primary school with a request to design and make some educational toys to help the children develop their numeracy skills.

Identifying the users and the intended market for the product

It is important to identify the **user** of the product.

In the above example, the children will use the product, that is the educational toys, but the teachers or other adults who may use the toys with the children should also be considered.

The **intended market** for the educational toys is the local primary school but this could be widened to include more than just one primary school.

Developing a design brief for a marketable product

The request from the primary school for educational toys would result in the following **design brief**:

Design and make an educational toy that could be used to help a 5-year-old learn about numbers.

Think about this design brief as you work through the next section on how to develop a specification to meet the brief.

Key words

The **user** is the person (or people) who will use the product.

The **intended market** is the range of people the designer considers to be potential buyers and/or users of the product.

A **design brief** explains clearly, in a short statement, the task that needs to be solved.

Key points

You must be able to:

- identify design problems from a variety of information sources
- identify the users and the intended market for products so that they can become marketable
- write a clear design brief, giving an outline of the problem to be solved or need to be satisfied.

Activity

Write a design brief for your coursework project.

a Explain how you identified the need or problem.

b Identify the user and the intended market for the product.

Drawing up a specification

This section will cover:

- Examining the intended purpose of the product.
- Identifying and collecting relevant data.
- Considering issues that affect planning.
- Identifying and evaluating existing products.
- Writing a specification.
- Manufacturing the product in batch quantity.

Before starting to draw your design ideas, you should write a **specification**. This means gathering information from various sources that will help you build up a picture of what the educational toy has to do, what it must look like, how it must work, its cost and how it will be produced.

Key word

A **specification** is a list of design points that can be used to guide your thinking when you start to draw and develop your design ideas.

Examining the intended purpose of the product

You will need to think about how the educational toy will be used. There are a number of ways to find this out:

- You could visit the primary school and observe the children working and playing in different environments.
- You could interview the teacher to find out how the children learn, what activities they like or what kind of toy might be most suitable.
- You could look at existing toys to see how effective they are.

Identifying and collecting relevant data

Think about the children who will use the educational toy. What kind of data would you need to find out? Consider the following:

- Anthropometric data, that is information on sizes of human beings such as height, reach or hand and arm dimensions, could be important to the design of the toy.
- Safety issues need to be considered. Products manufactured for use by children have to meet specific standards laid down by the British Standards Institute (BSI).
- It may be important to consider dimensions, for example the toys may have to be a specific size so that they will fit into a drawer for storage or be used alongside an existing piece of equipment.

Considering issues that affect planning

There are two main issues that you will need to think about:

- Costs, in terms of the materials you will use to make the toys and the method of production. These will have an impact on the final cost of the product. The primary school will want to buy the educational toys for a 'reasonable' price.

- Environmental issues, which include the choice of resources used for the toys. For example, are the resources renewable? Renewable resources include timber from sustainable forests; non-renewable resources include fossil fuels, some plastics and metals.

Identifying and evaluating existing products

Existing products are those designs that are already in use.

When looking at an existing product, you need to consider:

- Its purpose – how far does the product meet the original specification?
- The materials used and their suitability.
- The manufacturing processes involved.

Product analysis

Product analysis can be a starting point for your own design ideas.

Examining educational toys used by teachers with children will help you to answer some of the questions raised above. For example:

- It will be clear how the toy works and what it is supposed to do.
- By handling the toy, you will be able to see how the designer has considered **ergonomics**, for example whether or not it is the right size or comfortable to hold.
- The appearance of the product can be evaluated in terms of its appeal.
- The materials can be examined for their suitability.
- You may consider using particular materials because they can be recycled.
- The easing of corners, securely fixed parts and non-toxic finish will tell you that the toy is safe in use.

In addition, you may be able to recognise weak points in the design or consider how it could be manufactured in quantity.

Sometimes it may be necessary to disassemble a product to find out how it works.

Key words

Product analysis involves examining an existing product to try to work out why it was designed in a particular way.

Ergonomics is studying how efficiently people can work in an environment or use a product.

Writing a specification

Once you have carried out your research, considered it carefully and drawn conclusions about it, you are ready to write a specification. It is essential to use only the data that you think will definitely help in the design of the product. The specification will be a valuable tool at the end of the project when each of the criteria can be checked against the performance of the final product.

When developing a specification for an educational toy for a 5-year-old you would want to include the points below.

The educational toy must be:

- safe for children to use
- attractive and appealing to children
- made from quality, durable materials that are environmentally friendly
- capable of helping children develop confidence when using numbers
- economical to manufacture as one of a batch of 50 identical products.

Manufacturing the product in batch quantity

Batch production involves the manufacture of several to a few thousand identical products. In your coursework project you will have designed at least part of a product that could be batch produced.

Control systems

At this early stage in the design process it is important to think about possible control systems that could be used to make sure every educational toy is made to the same quality and accuracy. Some of the control systems used in your coursework include templates, jigs and formers. (See pages 19–22 for a description of this method of manufacture.)

Key points

You must be able to:

- explain the various ways to find out about the intended purpose of a product
- identify and collect relevant data including anthropometrics, dimensions and standards set by BSI
- explain that cost and environmental issues can affect planning
- carry out product analysis of existing products in order to evaluate their success
- write a clear and detailed specification to guide your design thinking
- explain how control systems are used to ensure accuracy during batch production.

Questions

1 You have been asked to design a magazine rack for the school library. Write down four questions you would need to ask the librarian when carrying out your research.

2 Identify and describe two pieces of important information you would need to find out before designing a desk-tidy.

3 Name two issues that can affect planning.

Activities

1 Carry out a product analysis of a can opener.
Ask yourself:
   - What materials have been used, and why?
   - How does the can opener work?
   - Are there any safety features?
   - How has the designer considered ergonomics in the design of the can opener?

2 Imagine that you have been asked to design a kitchen toaster. Think carefully about *how* it will be used and *what* it will look like. Write a specification for the toaster, including at least six design criteria.

Generating design proposals

This section will cover:

- Generating design proposals.
- Identifying resources.
- Evaluating ideas against the specification.
- Understanding the relevance of function and aesthetics.
- The use of modelling.

Your coursework project will already have introduced you to this section. While there are other stages and activities not listed above that you will have recorded in your folder, the ones covered here are the key areas on which you can expect to be examined.

Generating design proposals

Sketches and drawings

The questions in the written exam will require you to present design proposals through the use of freehand sketches and notes. Sometimes greater accuracy will be needed in your sketches, for example when sketching a particular mechanism or completing a drawing.

The drawings or 'figures' shown in the exam papers are presented in different ways. Most of them will be drawn three dimensionally (3D) but sometimes there will be two dimensional (2D) drawings and occasionally sectional views. It is important that you are familiar with the way the questions are presented to you.

Many of the questions involving design proposals carry several marks. In some of the specimen questions there can be from 2 up to a maximum of 8 marks for correct answers. Sometimes the question will 'break down' what you have to do. Within the 8 marks there could be separate marks for naming a material, construction and fitting. In some questions you will be given a specification listing three or four important points that have to be met. Marks would be awarded for how well you answer each of these.

Communication skills

Communication skills are important in presenting your design proposals. How well you communicate the ideas can affect your marks. Often mark schemes carry 1 or 2 marks for communication skills alone. Examiners' reports often comment on the need for more clarity and detail in answers. For some of these questions there could be at least half a page of space on the exam paper, and this should tell you that the examiner is expecting some large, clear sketches from you. You should use written notes to go with your design proposal sketches to explain detail that would otherwise be difficult to show by sketches.

Identifying resources

The questions will ask you to generate design proposals in a variety of ways. These include showing:

- **construction methods**
- **processes**
- **modifications needed**
- **materials and fittings**
- **jigs, formers** and **templates**.

Construction methods

A question might ask you to show how separate parts of a product could be joined together, for example, how the lower shelf of a bedside cabinet could be joined to the ends of a cabinet using suitable knock-down (KD) fittings.

Knock-down fittings are used to make furniture that can be taken apart so that it can be moved and reassembled later.

Processes

A question might ask you, for example, to describe how you could form the 90 degree bend in a metal bookend and name the tools and equipment used. A correct answer would describe how the metal could be held in a vice while being bent using a wooden mallet or a hammer with scrapwood.

Modifications needed

The question might ask for a modification to be carried out to the metal bookend so that it could be clipped to a shelf and have space for a self-adhesive subject label to be fitted to it. The original design must be **modified** to meet these new requirements. A good solution would be to extend the front edge of the bookend so that it could be bent over a shelf and provide the space needed to fit a self-adhesive label to it.

Materials and fittings

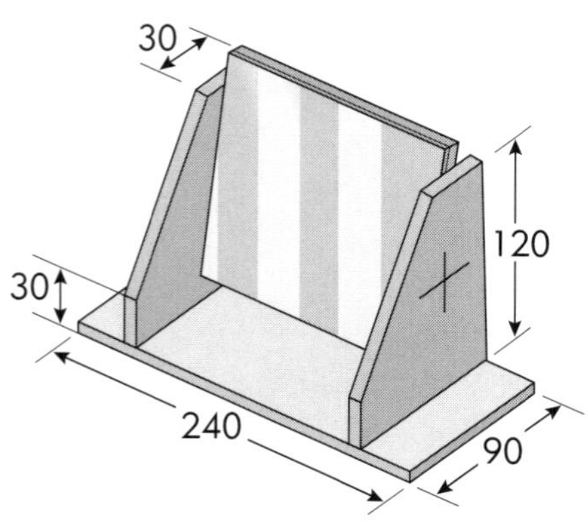

Sketch of an adjustable mirror.

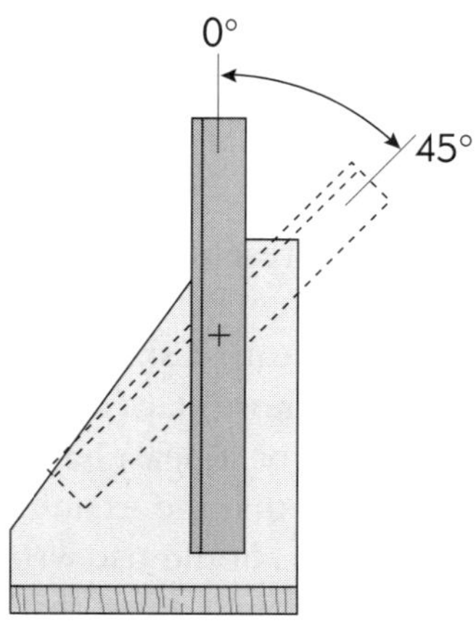

Key words

Construction method is the way that products are put together or formed or how separate parts of a product are joined together either temporarily or permanently.

A **process** is the way that a particular operation is carried out.

To **modify** a design means to change it for a particular purpose.

Materials are the resistant materials with which you will have worked during your D&T lessons: wood, metal and plastics.

Fittings refer to the type of hardware that you could use, for example screws, hinges, locks and fastenings.

Jigs, formers and **templates** are all used to help speed up the production process and maintain accuracy when manufacturing in quantity (see pages 19–22).

The question might ask you to name the materials and fittings used in a certain part of a product. The example above shows an adjustable mirror with a part that allows the mirror to pivot. In this example some type of screw could be used with a nut sunk into the edge of the mirror backing piece. A 'spacer' or washer could be inserted between the mirror and the uprights to allow for ease of movement.

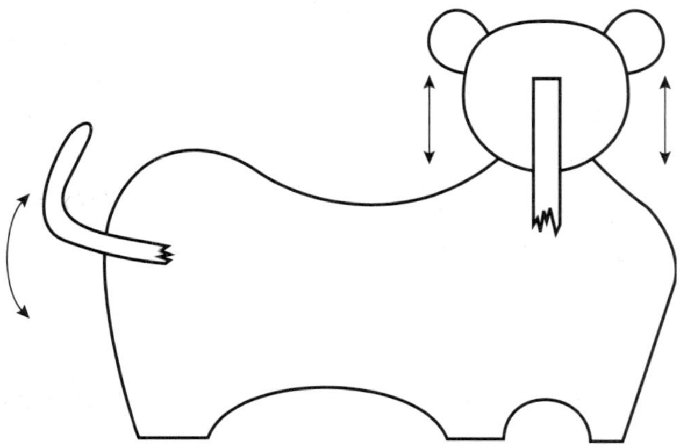

Reverse view of a hand-held toy.

This question might ask you to add details to a drawing of a mechanism, for example the hand-held toy above, that would make the head move up and down. In this example you would need to give details of connecting pieces and pivots and a method of controlling the distance moved by the head. One way of controlling the distance moved by the head would be to glue a small block of wood above or below the **linkage** attached to the tail to limit the distance it could move. A knowledge and understanding of linkages would enable you to answer this question correctly.

Key words

Linkage describes those parts of a machine or mechanism that connect moving parts together. They can also be used to control movement.

Evaluating means testing an idea to see how 'good' it is. It is a practical activity that uses the original specification to check whether or not the design criteria and original need have been met.

Jigs, formers and templates

The question might ask you to design one jig that would enable two different processes to be successfully carried out. For example, when making a set of wind chimes:

- sawing a metal tube to three different lengths
- drilling a 2 mm diameter hole in each length of tube.

With jigs of this kind it is important not to concentrate simply on the sawing and drilling processes but to consider how you would use the jig. For example, how would you make sure that the tube is held in position while it is being sawn and drilled? (The sawing jig shown on page 19 shows how the metal tube could be held in place.)

Evaluating ideas against the specification

Evaluating a design idea involves writing comments about it. These can include 'good' and 'bad' points about the design idea. It is important to be honest in your comments as these will also provide a starting point from which the design idea can be developed, modified and improved.

Understanding the relevance of function and aesthetics

Consider the **functional requirements** in the design of a rucksack. They would include the following:

- The most suitable material for the job. A rucksack is carried and used outdoors so the material for the frame would need to be lightweight, strong and resistant to corrosion.
- The type of finish that would be applied. This would need to be a hardwearing paint or industrial finish that would stand up to tough outdoor use and different weather conditions.
- The durability of the materials and constructions so that the product will last. Steel or aluminium with welded joints would be good functional choices.
- Ergonomic requirements such as how easy any clips or buckles are to fasten and undo or how easily the straps adjust.

Now consider the **aesthetic** features of a product. These would include its:

- colour
- shape
- form
- finish.

A designer usually needs to maintain a balance between function and aesthetics depending on the type of product. For example, while it is essential that a product such as a personal CD player works effectively, there is a considerable aesthetic influence within the design. However, with some products there is an imbalance. For example, a design for a piece of jewellery would concentrate more on aesthetics than function, while a design for a vacuum cleaner would concentrate more on function. In both examples there is still a need to consider both function and aesthetics.

Key words

Function is what a product does, how it works and how well it does it.

Functional requirements are those things that a product must have in order to work properly.

Key word

Aesthetics is to do with how a product looks.

The use of modelling

A **prototype** can be made at any stage in the design process to test or check a specific aspect of the design. Mock-ups are 'rough' models that are used at an early stage in the design process.

Models enable designers to:

- test whether the design will work
- check to see if the product can be put together properly
- look at the product in its specific environment
- check the sizes
- visualise exactly what the product will look like
- present their designs to potential customers or clients.

A model can also be used to prevent costly mistakes in terms of materials, time and labour later on during manufacture. It could be very costly to proceed with full-scale manufacture only to find that there were faults in the design.

It is not practical for you to make a model under exam conditions but it is possible to test your understanding of the importance and relevance of using mock-up models during your design work.

Key word

A **prototype** is a detailed full-scale model of a design produced prior to manufacture.

Key points

You must be able to:

- generate design proposals for a wide range of problems and situations
- identify the resources needed to manufacture a design proposal
- use a variety of communication skills effectively to explain your design proposals
- evaluate ideas against a specification and consider whether the specification meets the original need
- recognise the importance of function and aesthetics in product design
- understand the difference between a mock-up and a prototype model
- understand why models are used by designers and what they can tell us.

Questions

1 Look at the child's toy shown opposite.

Use sketches and notes to show two modifications to the design that would make it more interesting for a child to play with.

2 Explain why it would be an advantage to make the toy from two thin pieces of manufactured board rather than one thicker piece.

3 Look at the adjustable mirror on page 14. State two functional requirements that this product would need to meet.

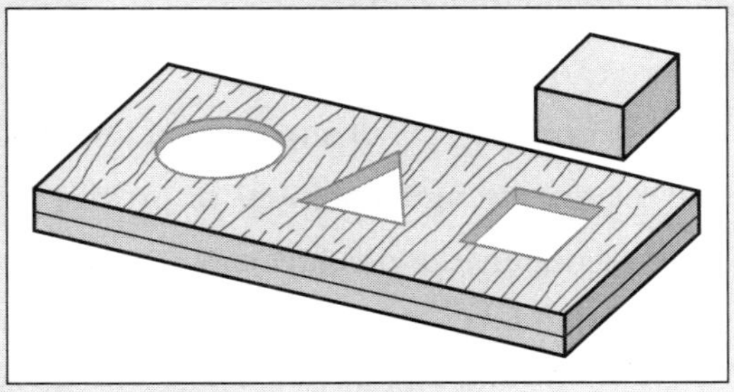

A child's toy.

Activities

1 Consider the following products:

- can opener
- camera
- kitchen clock
- photo frame.

Think about how far the designer has needed to consider aesthetics and function in the design of these products. Which is more important? Answer this question by marking an **X** for each product on the scales below. An example of a clothes peg has been done for you.

Product	**Function** ←→ **Aesthetics**
Clothes peg	←—X———————→
Can opener	←——————————→
Camera	←——————————→
Kitchen clock	←——————————→
Photo frame	←——————————→

2 Think carefully about the clothes peg, can opener, kitchen clock and photo frame in the table above. Why would you make a model of each of these products? What would it be for?

Product development

This section will cover:

- Testing and trialling.
- Developing a system to control the manufacture of a product.

Testing and trialling

Testing and trialling is carried out in order to find out the best materials to use, including pre-manufactured standard components and the best ways of manufacturing the product.

Tests are carried out to find out:

- how strong the overall structure of the product is
- the relative strengths of joints or processes that could be used
- how accurately the product can be made
- how long it takes to manufacture the product keeping cost in mind
- what the product looks like, especially the surface finish
- which components are the most suitable.

When choosing the most appropriate material for a product it is important to consider how the product will be made and the scale of manufacture, that is, is the product a one-off or will it be batch or even mass produced?

There are four ways of working with materials to consider when making decisions about manufacture:

- **deforming**
- **casting**
- **moulding**
- **wasting**.

Each of these methods is covered in more detail on pages 44–67.

The bookend described on page 14 is made from a single piece of metal and the production process needs to be appropriate for the material. Therefore the metal will be drilled, sawn and bent to shape. If the bookend were to be mass produced, it would be stamped out before being bent to shape. If the designer had chosen wood for the bookend, it would need to be **fabricated**.

Before making a decision about materials and processes to be used in the manufacture of the product, it is essential to test or trial them. With the bookend, this could mean choosing two different pieces of sheet metal, for example steel and aluminium, and striking them with a hammer and a piece of scrapwood in a vice to find out which was the easier to bend. Using the same two materials, tests could be carried out to give information about ease of sawing or drilling or quality of finishing.

Key words

Deforming involves changing the shape of a material by bending, forming or pressing.

Casting involves pouring molten metal or plastic into a mould.

Moulding involves heating plastic granules until soft before injecting them into a mould.

Wasting is changing the shape of the material by cutting pieces off it by filing, sawing, cutting, drilling or machining.

Since the majority of products are not made from single pieces of material it is necessary to join together and assemble separate pieces of the same or different materials. This is called **fabrication**.

If the bookend were to be made from wood, then the designer would need to find the most suitable type of joint for the product. Cutting out and assembling different joints enables the designer to understand the complexity of each joint and the time taken to make it. Tests could be carried out to find out the relative strength of each joint.

The adjustable mirror on page 14 requires some form of pivot and locking device to hold the mirror in different positions. There is a range of pre-manufactured standard components available, including screws and fastenings that could be used. Some of these will work or look better than others. It is important to test a variety before making a final decision.

Many of the processes covered in this section are discussed in more detail on pages 47–69.

Developing a system to control the manufacture of a product

You will have experience of jig design through your coursework project and you should apply this knowledge when answering the exam questions.

Jigs, formers and templates are used to speed up production when making products. They are used to do repetitive jobs and are useful because they:

- save time, so reducing production costs
- make sure every product is identical.

Jigs, formers and templates with specific uses are shown below. The 'good features' given for each device are what examiners are looking for in your answers in the exam.

Jigs

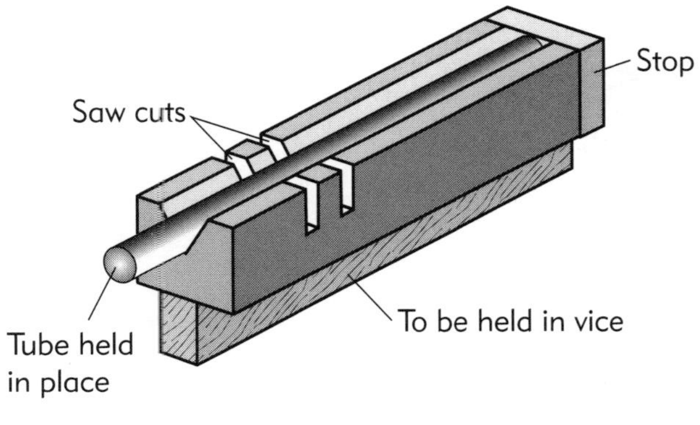

A sawing jig.

The sawing **jig** has several good features:

- The tube to be cut is held securely in place.
- Part of the jig can fit into a vice to prevent it from moving about.
- Identical lengths can be sawn due to the position of the saw cuts.
- It is easy to use.

Key word

Jigs are 3D devices that can be used to assist the manufacturing process when:

- sawing
- drilling
- bending and shaping.

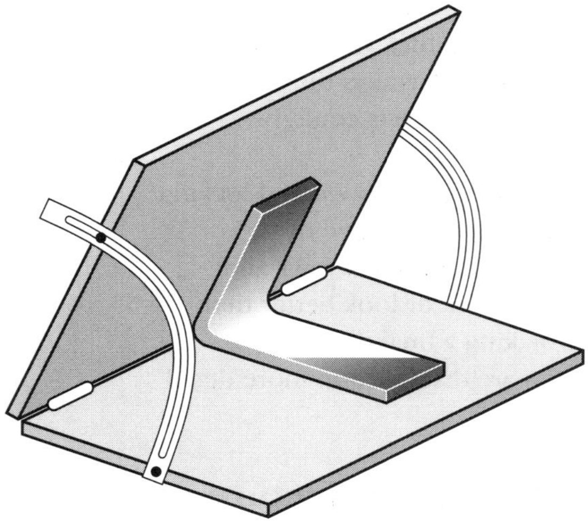

A bending jig.

The jig used to produce the internal (inside) bend in the sheet plastic has the following good features:

- It is adjustable to any angle between 0 and 90 degrees.
- It is quick and easy to adjust.
- The plastic can be pushed into the angle easily.
- The same angle can be achieved every time.

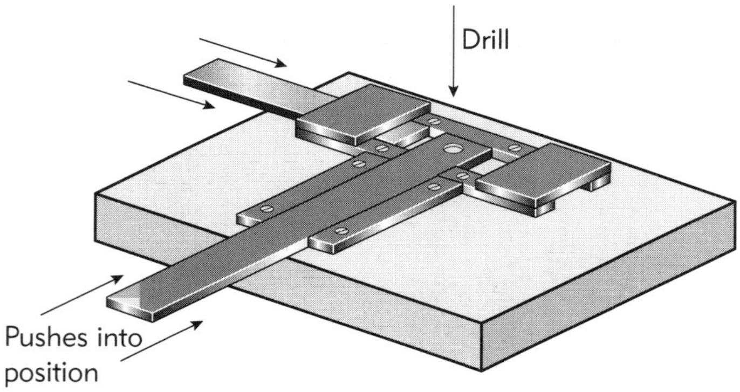

A drilling jig.

The drilling jig has the following good features:

- The jig fits quickly and easily over a drilling machine table.
- Strips of wood can be pushed into the jig and are held safely while being drilled.
- The holes can be drilled at the end of a strip or along its length depending on which 'guide' is used.
- The holes will be drilled in the same place every time.

Formers

Formers are used as a shape around which materials, often in sheet form, but sometimes in bar, rod or rectangular section, can be formed. Formers are also known as moulds. Many resistant materials such as plastics, including polystyrene and acrylic, when heated become soft and can be formed using moulds.

The following processes involve the use of formers or moulds:

- line bending
- press forming
- vacuum forming.

Line bending

Line bending is carried out by heating the plastic on a strip heater or line bender. The line bender heats a thin line along the plastic whereas a strip heater, with a wider heating element, heats a larger area of plastic.

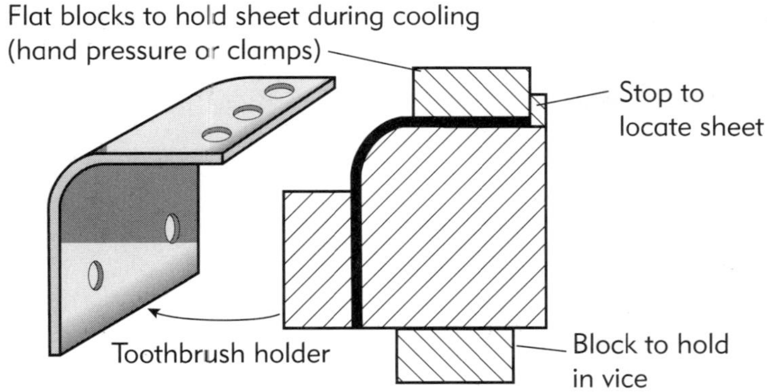

Bending metal around a former.

If the shape to be produced is wider than can be done by either of these methods, the plastic would be heated in an oven, then shaped around a former. In the example shown above, it is important to consider not only the final shape required but also how the plastic will be held in position while it is allowed to cool. It would be inefficient if the person bending the plastic had to hold it in position.

Press forming

Press forming involves male and female formers. The plastic sheet is first heated to make it soft, and is then sandwiched between the two formers. These are clamped together to provide the necessary pressure. Products such as shallow dishes and lids or covers can be made using this technique.

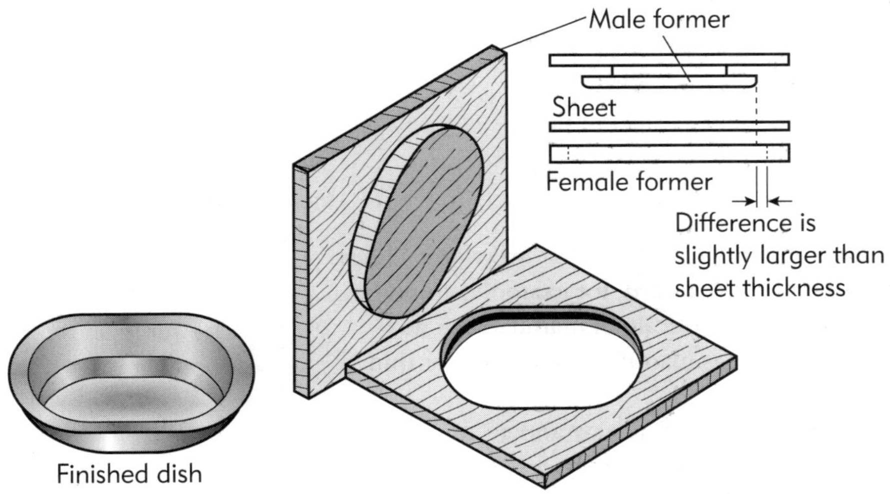

Press forming.

Vacuum forming

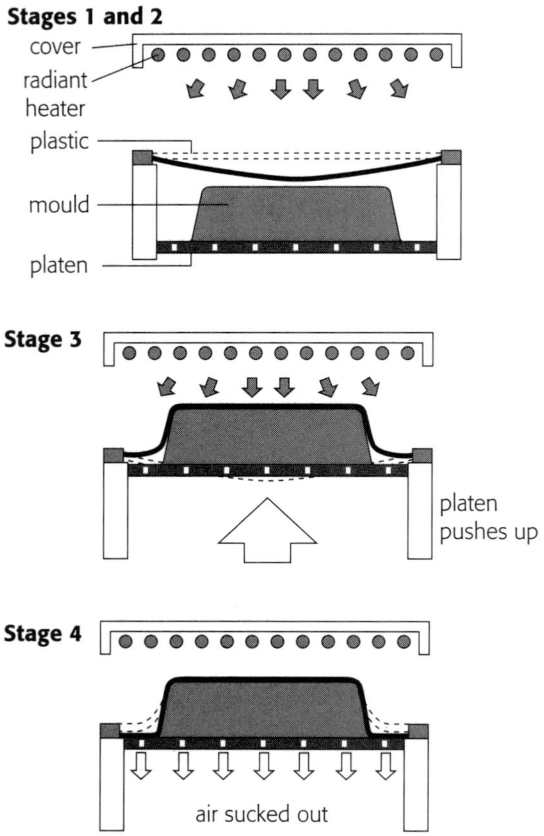

Vacuum forming.

Vacuum forming also involves the use of moulds around which a sheet of softened plastic can be shaped. The stages in vacuum forming are:

1 Place moulds on platen and lower.
2 Clamp sheet of polystyrene plastic in position.
3 Position heater over plastic sheet and heat to soften.
4 Remove heater, lift platen to push moulds into soft plastic and turn on pump to suck out the air.
5 Switch off pump and lower platen.
6 Release clamps and remove plastic sheet.

Templates

Often **templates** are the best way to mark out irregular or awkward shapes. Any thin, fairly rigid material is suitable. Thick card, for example, could be used to mark a small batch of products. If the scale of manufacture was larger, then a more durable material such as manufactured board or thin metal sheet would be better.

Using a template, a shape can be marked out quickly and accurately on sheet material. Some templates require greater accuracy, for example when marking out positions for constructions. In this case, it would be essential for the template to have some form of lipping that fitted up against at least two edges to ensure the correct location every time.

> ***Key word***
>
> **Templates** are useful for drawing the same shape many times.

Key points

You must be able to:

- explain why testing and trialling of materials, production processes and pre-manufactured standard components is essential
- give examples of the tests that could be carried out
- understand the difference between the manufacturing processes of deforming, casting, moulding and wasting
- give reasons why jigs, formers and templates are used in manufacturing
- explain the types of processes that use jigs, formers and templates
- describe important features of jigs used for sawing, drilling, bending and shaping and explain how they work
- identify, when examining a product, those parts of a product that could be manufactured using a jig, former or template
- design a jig, former or template for a specific purpose.

Questions

1 State two reasons for using a jig, former or template when manufacturing products.

2 Name three processes for which jigs may be used.

3 Describe three 'good' design features you would expect from a jig, former or template.

4 Toboggans can be made from moulded plastic or fabricated using hardwood. Explain the difference between the two processes.

5 State four reasons why you would carry out testing before deciding upon the method of manufacture of a product.

Activities

1 Think carefully about some of the products described on pages 14–15. During the manufacture of the following products explain where you could use either a jig, former or template:
   - a template for an adjustable mirror
   - a former for a metal bookend
   - a jig for a bedside cabinet.

2 Visit a local DIY store and find out information about dowel jigs. What are they used for?

3 Look carefully at the adjustable mirror on page 14 and describe four tests you could carry out before starting batch production.

Product planning

This section will cover:

- Producing detailed work plans.
- Preparing materials to allow for waste and fine finishing.

Producing detailed work plans

As in previous sections, you should be able to apply knowledge and understanding of planning from your internally assessed coursework project.

Working drawings and cutting lists

As a final design is developed, **working drawings** and a **cutting list** need to be produced. These should enable a different person to make the product without the need for discussion.

Working drawings may be presented as:

- views drawn in orthographic projection
- isometric views
- freehand or instrument-drawn views.

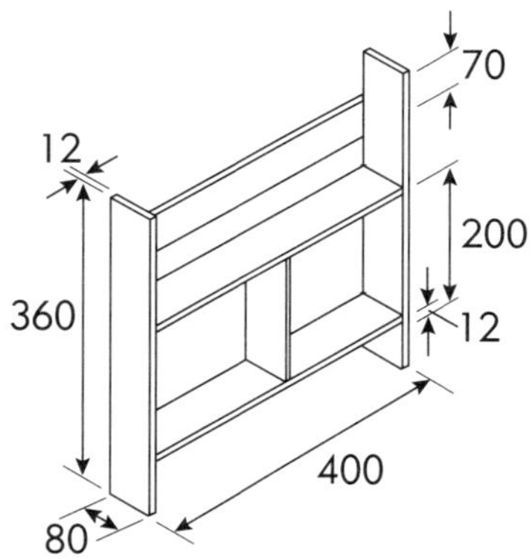

Working drawing of a wall-mounted rack.

An example of a cutting list is shown below.

Part name	Number required	Size (mm) (length × width × thickness)	Material
End	2	360 × 80 × 12	Mahogany
Shelf	2	400 × 80 × 12	Mahogany
Back rail	1	400 × 70 × 12	Mahogany
Upright	1	200 × 80 × 12	Mahogany

If any fittings are needed, these would be added to the list, for example screws and hinges.

Key words

Working drawings include all the details necessary to make the product.

A **cutting list** or parts list should include all the parts of the product, the type of materials to be used, their sizes and the quantities required.

Working drawings and cutting lists are an important part of practical work, but planning is an important area of the specification on which exam questions are set. These questions are usually presented as a table to be completed in one or two different ways:

- Describe a process that would be carried out at a particular stage.
- Name the tools or equipment that could be used to carry out a particular process.

The TV and hi-fi unit shown here is made from a manufactured board with a spray painted finish. It will be produced as a flat pack ready for home assembly.

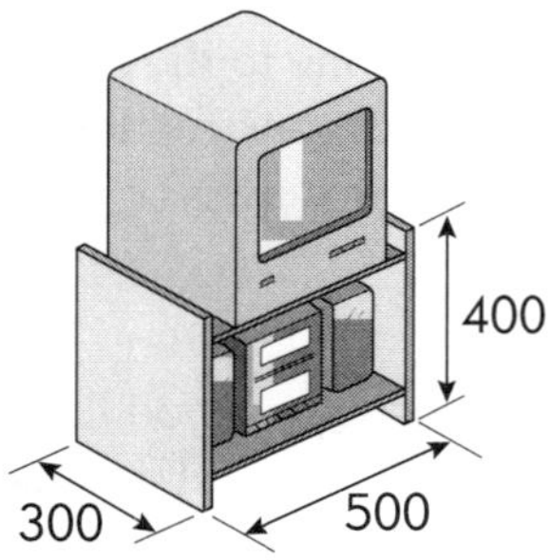

Working drawing of a television and hi-fi unit.

A **flow chart** to include many more details of the manufacture of a hi-fi unit would appear like this:

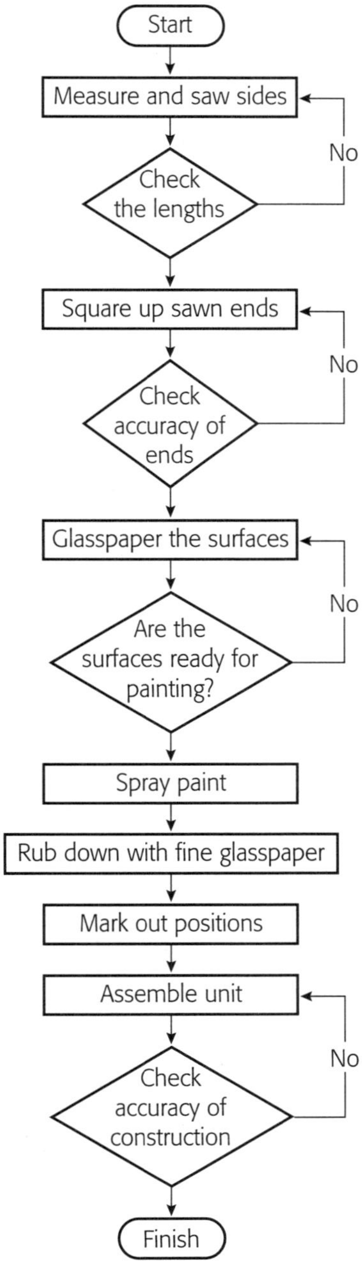

You may think of other stages that could be included in the flow chart.

Stages in the manufacture of a hi-fi unit.

Key word

Flow charts are used to show the order or sequence in which things happen. They include the following symbols:

Start/Finish

Operation or process

Decision

Preparing materials to allow for waste and fine finishing

It is important that the materials used to manufacture products are used economically with the minimum of waste. For example, wood has to be prepared by planing it to the required width and sawing it to length.

Material preparation is carried out with wood, metal and plastic. Preparation describes what needs to be done to the material to make sure it is flat, level or square before, for example, constructions can be carried out. Preparation is different for each of these materials.

Preparing wood

Sometimes it is necessary to plane or machine wood flat and square before any marking out can be done. After this, the wood is usually measured to length before sawing it.

Preparing metals

Metal is obtained in stock sizes and sections, including rod, bar, tubes and flats. Generally, there is no preparation necessary except for measuring and marking to length. The exception to this is where sheet material is needed and this would be marked with 'engineers blue', a blue ink, so that any marks made with a scriber are easy to read.

Preparing plastics

Sheet plastic is the most common form available. Marking can be difficult if using a scriber since it is hard to erase unwanted scribed lines on the face of the plastic. Instead, use a fine felt marker or a chinagraph pencil (a soft wax pencil suitable for marking on glass as well as plastic).

(For more on the processes and tools and equipment, see pages 54 and 61–2.)

Key points

You must be able to:

- produce a stage-by-stage detailed work plan
- include details of materials, fittings, tools and equipment used in manufacture
- read a working drawing and complete a cutting list
- produce a flow chart to show the order of processes involved in the manufacture of products
- show how you would mark out materials economically.

Questions

1 **Look at the drawing of the adjustable mirror below. It is to be made from separate pieces rather than one length of material.**

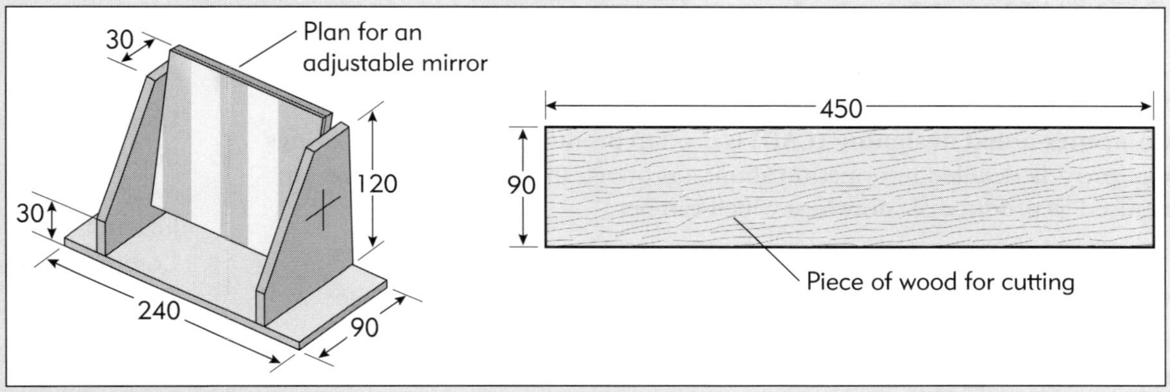

Drawing for an adjustable mirror.

a **Make a cutting list for this product.**

b **Show how the pieces for the sides and base could be marked out from the piece of wood shown.**

2 **Describe five main stages in the assembly of the wall-mounted rack shown on page 24. Assume that all the parts have been cut to length and have been prepared.**

Activities

a Select a child's wooden pull-along toy and produce a flow chart explaining the stages in which the item would have been manufactured.

b Make a cutting list for the same item. Include any fittings needed.

ICT applications

This section will cover:

- CAD/CAM used in industrial manufacturing.
- The use of computer systems to control machines and equipment.
- CAD/CAM used in the manufacture of single items and small batches.
- The advantages of CAD/CAM.
- The use of ICT to aid Design and Technology activities.

CAD/CAM used in industrial manufacturing

CAD

Computer-aided designing (CAD) is used to produce 2D working drawings that provide detailed information about a product. In addition, software can be used to produce 3D drawings which can be:

- rotated on screen to enable the product to be viewed from all angles
- made to appear as if manufactured from different materials or surface finishes
- sectioned
- enhanced by different camera angles or background lighting
- animated on screen, that is, made to move as intended to enable the designer to see if it will actually work.

Such software enables designers to present 'virtual' products to potential customers.

CAD/CAM

CAD/**CAM** describes the process that links computer-aided designing with computer-aided manufacture. The computer recognises a design drawing as numerical data. This data is processed and converted into specific data that can be transferred to and understood by the machines used to manufacture the product.

CNC

Computer numerical control is the system used to process the data from the design drawing to the machine used to manufacture the product. There is a range of **CNC** machines that are used in CAM including: lathe, milling machine, engraver, router and vinyl cutters.

Key word

Computer-aided design (CAD) means using Information and Communication Technology (ICT) at any stage in the design process to help develop the design of a product.

Key words

Computer-aided manufacture (CAM) involves the use of a computer system to assist in the manufacture of products. This can include marketing, stock control, quality control and robot assembly systems.

CNC stands for computer numerical control.

Rapid Prototyping

Think of a **Rapid Prototyping** machine as a printer but instead of it producing a 2D design on paper, it will produce layer upon layer that eventually grows into a 3D model.

Rapid Prototyping machines are very expensive and companies do not purchase their own machines. They employ specialist companies to do the job for them.

The system produces prototypes very quickly. This reduces costs for companies because the prototype can be tested and evaluated and modifications made before starting full-scale production.

Key word

Rapid Prototyping allows 3D computer-generated design drawings to be produced as actual 3D models.

The use of computer systems to control machines and equipment

Components and materials need to be moved between processes and onto and off machines. Delays during manufacture can be very costly to companies. Robotics is an effective and simple computer-operated system.

Robotics

A robot arm is able to pick up and position objects. A computer is used to instruct the robot arm. Sensors on the arm inform the computer when it has moved into position.

Robots can be used on large-scale projects such as spray-painting a vehicle or for much simpler jobs such as inserting components into an electronic circuit board.

Advantages of using robots:

- They carry out boring and repetitive jobs that would have to be carried out by people.
- They can carry out jobs in dangerous or uncomfortable conditions.
- They can be relied upon for great repetitive accuracy.
- They can be reprogrammed quickly, making them flexible and adaptable.

CAD/CAM used in the manufacture of single items and small batches

Many of the principles used in industrial CAD/CAM can be applied on a smaller scale to the manufacture of single items or batches in school. It is very important that you understand the main stages in setting up the machines used to manufacture products.

Example 1

For example, CAD/CAM could be used in a school-based project to design and manufacture a child's educational game which requires that numbers and dots are marked onto the sides of cube blocks. The numbers and dots are made from self-adhesive vinyl. Appropriate software to design the numbers and dots would be Techsoft 2D Design. A Roland CAMM1 machine linked to the computer could be used to cut the numbers and dots professionally.

There are various stages involved in the manufacturing process after the colour of the vinyl has been chosen:

1 Set up the vinyl in the CAMM1 and clamp in position.
2 Type in onscreen instructions for the computer to send information to the CAMM1, including:
    - the number of passes (cuts) that are needed to cut through the vinyl but not the backing sheet
    - the speed at which the cutter moves and therefore cuts the vinyl.
3 Adjust the pressure that the cutter makes as it cuts by moving a sliding switch.

The process is very quick. The vinyl would be removed from the machine and a further number of operations would be carried out by hand resulting in the completion of the numbers and dots ready to be applied to the wooden blocks.

Example 2

A second example of using CAD/CAM in a school-based project involves the designing and making of a small key fob made from a 2 mm-thick plastic laminate. The key fob could be designed using Techsoft 2D Design and cut and engraved by means of a Roland CAMM2 machine linked to the computer. There are more settings or tool parameters to consider than with the CAMM1 because the CAMM2 cuts or engraves along three axes: X, Y and Z. The X axis is along the bed of the machine from left to right; the Y axis from front to back; and the Z axis is the vertical distance or depth up and down.

The main stages include the following:

1 Secure the plastic to the bed of the machine using double-sided tape.
2 Insert the correct diameter and type of tool into the CAMM2 machine and enter the required settings into the machine.
3 Set the tool parameters for the CAMM2 by typing the following information into the computer:
    - The final depth of cut. On a piece of 2 mm-thick plastic there could be two depths to set – the depth of any engraving that is to be carried out to the surface of the plastic and the depth to cut through the material (in this case 2 mm).
    - The maximum depth of cut per pass. The type of material to be cut and the diameter of the tool would need to be considered when setting this. The 2 mm-thick plastic would need to have each depth of pass no more than 0.5 mm so it would cut the plastic four times to achieve the final depth of 2 mm.
    - The clearance of the tool as it passes over the plastic. The tool only needs to clear or pass above the surface of the plastic by 1 or 2 mm.
    - The diameter of the tool being used also needs to be set.
    - The speed that the tool moves along the three axes, X, Y and Z. The horizontal feed is the speed along the X and Y axes, while the vertical feed is the speed the tool makes as it cuts to depth vertically along the Z axis. The speeds depend on the material being cut and the diameter of the tool being used.

4 The CAMM2 machine will now carry out the manufacturing process and the material can be removed from the bed of the machine.

There are different makes of machines that carry out similar functions. The tool parameters discussed are common to all these machines.

The advantages of CAD/CAM

CAD

- Computers can be used to make changes to a design very quickly.
- Computers can be used to produce very accurate drawings and modify them without having to redraw them.
- Computers can produce photo-realistic models without having to make them.
- Computers can show or simulate how a product will behave without having to undertake expensive testing.
- Computers enable information to be accessed across the world.
- A large amount of information can be stored in a very small space.

CAM

- Computers do not get tired or bored like human beings.
- Computers do not make mistakes if programmed properly.
- Computers can control a number of machines at the same time.
- Computers give reliable and consistently high standards of manufacture.
- Computers can be used to monitor the quantity of stock or components required to manufacture products.
- Computers can operate in hazardous conditions where human beings could not work safely.
- Computers achieve quicker production times. Complex shapes and designs can be created easily.

The use of ICT to aid Design and Technology activities

In addition to CAD/CAM there are other ways that ICT can be used to help with the development of design proposals:

Databases

- When carrying out research for a project a **database** can be a valuable source of information. For example, a school database could be used to find out how many elderly people live in a particular area. This could be important when carrying out a questionnaire or survey connected to your project.
- The Internet is a powerful research tool, especially when researching topics where information in the form of books or magazines is not easily available. The Internet enables you to access information from all over the world.

> ***Key word***
> A **database** is a method of storing information in a way that enables the user to compare different pieces of information.

Spreadsheets

The information in a database can be displayed using a **spreadsheet**. By using mathematical formulae a spreadsheet program can calculate such things as costings. Detailed information such as all the materials required for a product, their sizes, quantities and costs could be entered onto a spreadsheet. Tables and charts to show information can be created quickly from the spreadsheet.

Key word

A **spreadsheet** is a type of chart that displays large amounts of information.

Desktop publishing

Desktop publishing software enables you to create professional looking pages of text with diagrams, photos, tables and charts. This can greatly improve the presentation of your work.

Key points

You must be able to:

- explain the difference between CAD and CAM and how they work
- explain what is meant by CNC and name a variety of CNC machines
- explain what is meant by Rapid Prototyping and why companies use it
- explain how industry uses robotics and what advantages they have in manufacturing
- explain how CAD/CAM is used in school to produce one-off and small-batch production
- describe the main stages involved in CAM processes in school-based projects
- explain how ICT can assist Design and Technology activities.

Questions

1 Describe four important features of CAD software.
2 Why are computer-controlled machines known as CNC machines?
3 Give two reasons why Rapid Prototyping is important to industry.
4 State two advantages of using robots in industry.
5 Describe three tool settings that need to be made to a CAMM2 machine before machining is started.

Activities

1 Find three products in your home that could have been manufactured by means of robots.
2 Choose a product that you have made at school. Consider how it could be designed and manufactured in quantity using CAD/CAM.
3 Use the Internet to find out about the bicycle stands used to carry out maintenance that are currently on the market.

Industrial applications

This section will cover:

- Commercial production methods, including:
  - one-off or job production
  - batch production
  - repetitive flow production
  - continual flow production.
- Commercial manufacturing systems, including:
  - cell production
  - in-line assembly
  - just-in-time
  - logistics.
- Quality assurance and quality control.

Commercial production methods

One-off or job production

One-off production or **job production** means the product could be made from start to finish by either one person or by a group of people, each working on a separate part of the same item. The product will be unique. Because it is labour intensive, it is a very expensive way of manufacturing products. A single item that you have made in your school workshop would be an example of one-off production.

Batch production

Batch production is where products are made by a group of people sharing tasks and equipment. The group may need to be flexible and be able to change quickly from the manufacture of one product to a different one.

In your internally-assessed coursework project you will have designed at least part of a product with the intention that it could be batch produced.

Repetitive flow production

An example of **repetitive flow production** is children's toys. The production is usually broken down into sub-assemblies of smaller components. This form of production can be labour intensive or completely automated, depending on the type of product being manufactured. The cost of a product decreases as the number of products that are manufactured increases.

Continual flow production

Very often **continual flow production** operates 24 hours a day, seven days a week as it is expensive to shut down and then restart machinery. Injection-moulded plastic garden furniture is an example of a product made by this process. There are fewer people involved than on an assembly line. It is essential that machinery is well-maintained to avoid breakdowns and any interruption to the production process that would be costly.

Key words

One-off production or **job production** means a single item made to the customer's specification.

Batch production refers to the manufacture of anything from several to a few thousand identical products.

Repetitive flow production means the manufacture of large quantities of identical products for a relatively low cost.

Continual flow production involves the manufacture of a finished product from raw materials which may have to be processed in some way.

Commercial manufacturing systems

Cell production

Some electrical goods such as vacuum cleaners would be produced by **cell production**. The workstations involved in the production process may carry out different tasks, for example machining, assembling or quality control inspection. The cell may be fully automated or have a team of people with a team leader.

In-line assembly

In-line assembly is used to mass produce many everyday items such as cars. Often a conveyor belt is used. One advantage of this system is that it can be fully automated with only a few semi-skilled people needed to supervise the operation.

Just-in-time

Deliveries of materials, components and sub-assemblies may be made several times a day to ensure production runs smoothly. Once completed, products are despatched immediately. The advantages of this system are that there is no need for storage facilities and changes to products can be made without having to use up all existing stock first. One disadvantage of this system is that late deliveries cause expensive delays.

Logistics

Logistics is the system used by the manufacturing industry to make sure that all the materials and components needed for production are available when required.

Key words

Cell production refers to the use of a number of workstations grouped together to produce a single component or a number of similar components.

In-line assembly is a system whereby components are added one at a time to make the finished product.

Just-in-time systems require all the materials, components and sub-assemblies to arrive from other factories at the exact time or 'just in time' for assembly.

Quality assurance and quality control

Achieving quality

Manufacturers try to produce quality products. The quality achieved will be judged against customer's needs, their expectations and the specification which the product must meet.

A company needs to achieve quality in manufacture because it can:

- reduce production costs by minimising waste and lost time
- improve the company's efficiency by making fewer faulty goods
- increase company profits
- improve the company's reputation.

Codes of practice

Codes of practice have been established in order to inform customers that **quality control** has been carried out to a certain standard and agreed specification. Many countries have their own codes. There are European and International codes, too. BS is the British Standard, ISO the International Standard and CEN the European Standard. One of the main bodies that promotes quality is the British Standards Institute (BSI). There are more than 10,000 British Standards covering a wide variety of products.

Key word

Quality Control is about inspecting and/or testing parts of a product or the production system in order to meet agreed quality standards.

Quality assurance concerns all aspects of a company's manufacturing performance from the design of a product, through its manufacture and including delivery.

Total quality management

Total quality management (TQM) means that everyone in a company has responsibility for achieving and maintaining high standards, whether it involves the design, manufacture or delivery of the products.

Inspection and testing

Inspection is where the product and the materials used are examined to see if they meet the agreed standards, including:

- accuracy to size
- overall appearance
- quality of surface finish
- quality and consistency of the materials.

Testing is concerned with the functional aspects of the product:

- Does the product do what it is supposed to do?
- Will it maintain this performance over a period of time?
- Will it be able to function in different environments?

The limits of **tolerance** are best established after testing or trialling of the product has been carried out. Tolerance levels are expressed by two numbers, an upper and a lower limit. For example, a component that has an agreed length of 100 mm but may vary between 99.4 mm and 100.6 mm is said to have a tolerance of + or – 0.6 mm. The tolerance is the difference between the upper and lower limits, that is, 1.2 mm or + or – 0.6 mm.

The precision involved in the manufacture of a plastic bucket would not need to be as great as for an intricate plastic switch for a computer. It would be a waste of time and money to work towards the highest level of accuracy if the product could function perfectly within greater tolerances.

> ***Key word***
>
> **Tolerance** describes the extent to which the size of the product can vary from its agreed sizes or dimensions.

Quality symbols

Quality symbols are used by manufacturers to inform customers of product standards. For example:

- The kite mark on some BSI products tells the customer that the product has been tested to destruction to ensure that it meets certain safety standards.
- The lion mark represents toy safety and quality. Toy manufacturers who sign a strict code of practice with the British Toy and Hobby Association (BTHA) are giving assurances about quality, safety and advertising standards. To display the lion mark means that their products conform to British Standard BSEN 71.

The BSI kite mark.

The lion mark.

Key points

You must be able to:

- identify the commercial production methods used in the manufacture of a wide range of products
- explain what is meant by one-off, batch, repetitive flow and continual flow production methods
- explain what is meant by commercial manufacturing systems including cell production, in-line assembly, just-in-time and logistics
- explain what is meant by quality assurance
- explain what is meant by the term 'total quality management' (TQM)
- explain what is meant by the term 'quality control' and how it may be carried out
- explain the meaning of the term 'tolerance' when applied to component sizes
- recognise two different quality symbols and explain what they stand for.

Questions

1 Name the type of production method you would choose to manufacture the following products: television sets, plate glass, pottery mugs, a pair of hand-made earrings. Give a reason for each of your choices.

2 Explain why one-off production is the most expensive production method.

3 Explain one possible disadvantage of the just-in-time manufacturing system.

4 Give three reasons why companies need to build quality assurance and control into their manufacturing systems.

Activities

1 Think carefully about your internally assessed coursework project.

   a Identify the best time to check accuracy of the product during manufacture.

   b Explain two tests that could be carried out during manufacture to ensure a quality product.

   c If you were to manufacture 1000 identical products, how could this be organised using a repetitive flow production method?

2 Consider the following products: washing machine, children's constructional toy, personal CD player, office swivel-chair. Make a list of tests that could be carried out during manufacture to ensure a quality product.

Product evaluation

This section will cover:

- Evaluating a product against an original specification.
- Evaluating a product against moral, cultural or environmental issues.
- Reviewing resources used to manufacture a product.
- Testing a product to find out how it could be improved.
- Evaluating the control system used to manufacture a product in order to find out how efficiently it has performed.

The work in this section is mainly concerned with the final evaluation of your internally assessed coursework project, but the activities involved can easily be applied to products that have been manufactured as a one-off or mass produced.

Evaluating a product against an original specification

During the earlier stages of the design of a product you would have carried out research and drawn conclusions as to the exact purpose, nature, appearance, and so on, of the product. The design criteria you listed are the elements which make up the specification.

When the product has been manufactured it is essential that you use the original specification as a checklist to assess the success of the product.

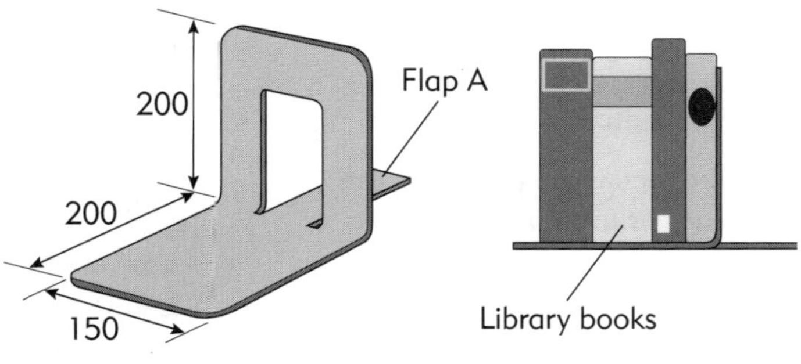

Design for a metal bookend.

A specification for the bookend shown above would include the following criteria:

- It must be stable in use.
- It must not fall over in use.
- It must safely support books that are placed against it. The books will rest on the base of the bookend and lean against the upright. They should not fall over.

- It should be economical to produce. The bookend is to be made from a single piece of sheet metal. There will be very little waste and the manufacturing processes are quick and efficient.
- It must be safe to handle, with no sharp edges or corners. Clearly, the corners have been rounded but you can only assume that the edges have been eased.

You may think of other important specification points for the bookend that could be evaluated in this way.

Evaluating a product against moral, cultural or environmental issues

Some people argue that it is wrong to allow children to play with toy guns because they believe it promotes violent behaviour. They criticise the toy manufacturers for making the guns. This is a **moral issue**. In the case of the bookend, there are no moral issues.

Designers also need to be sensitive to **cultural differences**. For example, furniture needs and styles for the Japanese who sit on the floor to eat and drink are very different to those in the UK. In addition, many religions celebrate special festivals while Jehovah's Witness celebrate none. Clearly, there are no cultural issues involved with the bookend.

Many products in the packaging industry are examples of **planned obsolescence**. Many electrical products that could be made to a higher specification are built to last only a limited time. There are arguments for and against planned obsolescence.

For a product to be 'environmentally friendly', it must do minimal harm to the environment during its manufacture, during its life span or when it is disposed of. If the bookend was made from steel or aluminium, then both metals could be recycled and the effects on the environment would be negligible. Designers must be aware of these **environmental issues**.

The bookend on page 37 can be evaluated in terms of environmental issues as follows:

- The raw materials from which it is made are plentiful.
- Mining or quarrying the ores from which the metals are produced can harm the environment by creating subsidence or unsightly landmarks such as quarries.
- Modern, efficient production methods using little energy should not affect the environment.
- Melting down and recycling the metal bookend when it is disposed of will help sustain resources.

Key words

Moral issues are to do with what people consider to be right and wrong.

Cultural issues are to do with the different values and beliefs held by people of differing nationalities, religions or ethnic origin.

Planned obsolescence is where a product is designed specifically to last over a period of time before it has to be replaced.

Environmental issues are to do with the effects a product may have on the environment in which we live.

Reviewing resources used to manufacture a product

Resources could include the materials, fittings and fixings, glue, polish or paint, tools, equipment and machinery. The following are examples of some of the resources **reviewed** in the manufacture of the bookend:

- Sheet metal such as mild steel is a good choice since it is fairly cheap and easy to work. Aluminium would also be a good choice as it is more flexible and lighter in weight making it easier to bend, and doesn't need painting. However, it is more expensive.
- Alternative materials could also be reviewed. Wood-based materials such as pine or plywood could be used, but these would be made from pieces that would need to be fabricated (joined). This would increase time and labour costs.
- Having chosen metal, it would be marked out with appropriate tools, the flap would have been drilled and sawn to shape. These processes are suitable, and if carried out accurately would result in a successfully shaped bookend. However, if an industrial press was available, the bookend could be made more quickly and accurately.
- The 90 degree bend could be achieved by hand by bending the metal around a wooden former and striking it with a hammer and piece of scrapwood. A bending machine would produce the bend quicker and more accurately.
- The edges of the metal would be filed smooth, edges rounded and cleaned before painting. Spray painting would achieve a better quality finish than most hand-painted finishes.

Testing a product to find out if it could be improved

Testing is used to find out information about the product, the materials it is made from, the construction, manufacturing processes and finish. The results of testing must be recorded and examined carefully since the main purpose of testing is not only to evaluate the success of the product but to make any necessary improvements to it.

Testing 'in situ'

There is only a certain amount of information that can be obtained by looking at a product while carrying out an evaluation. To obtain more information, it is a good idea to test the product under the same conditions, as far as possible, in which it will function. In the case of the bookend, collect a variety of different sized books, position the bookend on a flat surface similar to a bookshelf and prop up the books against the bookend. The points listed earlier in the specification can now be checked first hand. Is it stable? Does it support the books? Is it safe to handle?

Trialling

With other products it could be essential to find a suitable user to try out the product. For example, a toy could be given to a child and the way in which the toy is used could be observed, or a prototype for a new tool could be given to 20 employees who would be asked to trial the tool before completing a questionnaire about its effectiveness.

Some tests could take a while to produce a result. For example, a product that may be exposed to the weather would need to be exposed to a variety of conditions over a period of time. Similarly, durability tests to determine how hardwearing a product is could take longer and with school-based projects may be impractical.

Key words

Resources are all the things needed to make a product.

Review means to examine carefully whether or not the resources used were the most appropriate to make the product.

Evaluating the control system used to manufacture a product

Control systems are discussed in detail in Knowledge and Understanding, pages 72–8.

You will have designed a control system to be used in the manufacture of your product in the internally assessed coursework project. Imagine that the bookend has been designed and made as a prototype in a school workshop. A batch of 50 identical bookends are to be manufactured.

Systems are a series of components, operations or activities that, when joined together, enable a specific task to be carried out. The system in this case is designed to make the processes involved in the manufacture of the bookend easier, more efficient and accurate. Control is the means by which the system is managed.

Processes

First, you need to consider the processes involved in the manufacture of the bookend. They include:

- marking out
- sawing
- bending
- drilling
- filing
- cleaning and finishing.

Control systems

Then consider the control systems that are appropriate to these processes. Of the six processes listed above, three could be carried out in a school workshop – marking out, drilling and bending.

- Marking out could be done quickly and accurately by drawing around a template made to the shape of the 'net' of the bookend (see page 37). Marking out tools such as a steel rule and try square would therefore not be needed. A hole needs to be drilled in the sheet metal to allow a saw blade to be inserted so that the bookend can be sawn to shape. The template could include a drilled hole enabling the position for the hole to be marked out quickly and accurately.
- Instead of marking the position for the hole, the template could be designed to 'clip' over or locate onto the sheet metal securely and safely while the hole is drilled by a drilling machine. The template has doubled its function by becoming a drilling jig.
- In order to bend the sheet metal to the required shape, the metal would be held between folding bars in a vice. A hammer and scrapwood or a soft-faced hammer or mallet would be used to bend the metal. A wooden former held in a vice could also be used. This would ensure that a 90 degree bend was achieved every time. This would be an example of a bending jig.

Accuracy and efficiency

The main purpose of the control system when manufacturing in quantity is that it results in speed and repetitive accuracy. Examine each of the control systems used in the manufacture of the bookend and evaluate them:

- As long as the template has been produced and used accurately, it will prove to be successful.
- Similarly, if the hole is drilled in the correct position and the template or drilling jig can be located accurately, it will work well.
- The bending jig does rely on the force applied by a hammer or mallet to bend the metal to shape, but it is the folding bars or wooden former that achieves the correct 90 degree angle.

Key points

You must be able to:

- evaluate a product against its original specification
- consider moral, cultural and environmental issues when evaluating products
- evaluate the resources used in the manufacture of a product
- explain why and how products could be tested
- evaluate the performance of a control system used when manufacturing in quantity.

Questions

1. Explain why a detailed specification is needed when evaluating the success of a product.
2. Describe three ways in which designers and manufacturers of products can help the environment.
3. Give two advantages of using sheet metal rather than wood for the design of the bookend on page 37.
4. Explain the main purpose of:
   - **a** carrying out tests on products
   - **b** a manufacturing control system.

Activities

1. **a** Draw up a list of criteria that could be used to evaluate:
   - **i** a vacuum flask
   - **ii** a battery-powered torch.

   b Work out a series of practical tests you would carry out to evaluate them.
2. Write down the advantages and disadvantages of designing and making products that have only a limited life-span.
3. Consider a product that you made at school. Make a list of any environmental, moral and cultural issues you would need to consider if your product were to be manufactured in quantity.

Knowledge and Understanding

Materials and pre-manufactured standard components

This section will cover:

- Definitions of properties.
- Metals.
- Wood and wood-based materials.
- Plastics and composites.
- 'Smart' and modern materials.
- Using pre-manufactured standard components.
- Effects of pollution, waste and recyclability on society.

This section will help you to:

- identify a particular material for a particular situation
- identify the properties needed by a material to fulfil a particular purpose
- explain the effects on society of using materials in terms of pollution, waste and recycleability.

Definitions of properties

Properties are those characteristics or features of a material that makes it useful. It is important that when discussing materials these terms are used accurately.

The following terms are used to describe specific properties of materials:

- Hardness – is the extent to which a material resists cutting and surface indentation.
- Toughness – is the ability to withstand sudden shocks (the opposite of being brittle).
- Tensile strength – is the ability to withstand being pulled apart, crushed, twisted or subjected to a shear (sideways) force.
- Malleability – is the ability to be hammered into shape without breaking.
- Ductility – is the ability to be stretched (like wire) without breaking.
- Elasticity – is the ability to be stretched and then return to the original length.
- Thermal and electrical conductivity – is the extent to which the material can conduct heat and electricity.

Metals

There are two 'families' of metals:

- Ferrous – metals contain iron, for example steel.
- Non-ferrous – metals do not contain iron, for example aluminium, copper and brass.

Common ferrous metals

Metal	Composition	Properties	Uses
Mild steel	**Alloy** of iron and 0.15–0.30% carbon	High tensile strength, ductile, tough, fairly malleable, poor resistance to corrosion	General purpose, nails, screws, girders, car bodies
High carbon steel	0.70–1.40% carbon	Hardest of the carbon steels. Less ductile, tough or malleable	Hammers, chisels, screwdrivers
Medium carbon steel	0.30–0.70% carbon	Stronger and harder than mild steel but less ductile, tough and malleable	Garden tools, springs
Cast iron	Remelted pig iron with additions	Hard skin but brittle soft core. Strong under compression but cannot be bent or forged	Heavy crushing machines, car engines, machine parts
Stainless steel	Alloy of steel with 18% chrome and 8% nickel	Resistant to corrosion, hard, tough. Difficult to work	Sinks, dishes, cutlery
High speed steel	Medium carbon steel with tungsten, chromium, vanadium	Retains hardness at high temperatures. Can only be re-ground	Drills, lathe cutting tools
High tensile steel	Low carbon steel with nickel and chrome	Extremely hard and tough	Gears, shafts, engine parts, turbine blades

Key word

Alloys are mixtures of two or more pure metals or one or more pure metals mixed with other elements to create specific properties.

Common non-ferrous metals

Metal	Composition	Properties	Uses
Aluminium	Pure metal	High strength-weight ratio, light, soft, ductile, malleable, can be welded, good conductor of heat and electricity, corrosion resistant	Aircraft bodies, saucepans, cooking utensils, packaging, foils, cans, window frames
Copper	Pure metal	Malleable, ductile, tough, good conductor of heat/ electricity, easily joined, corrosion resistant	Electrical wire, hot water tanks, central heating pipes
Brass	Alloy of 65% copper, 35% zinc	Corrosion resistant, heat and electrical conductor, easily joined	Castings, ornaments, boat fittings
Bronze	Alloy of 90% copper, 10% tin	Tough, hardwearing, corrosion resistant	Bearings, castings for statues, coins
Gilding metal	Alloy of 85% copper, 15% zinc	Corrosion resistant, solders easily, attractive golden colour	Beaten metalwork, jewellery, architectural metalwork
Lead	Pure metal	Very soft, heavy, malleable, corrosion resistant, low melting point	Soft solders, roof coverings, protection against x-ray radiation
Tin	Pure metal	Soft, weak, low melting point, corrosion resistant	Coating as tinplate, soft solders
Zinc	Pure metal	Poor strength–weight ratio, low melting point, extremely corrosion resistant, easily worked	Coating (galvanising) steel, e.g. watering cans, dustbins, intricate die-castings

Market forms

There is a wide range of standard sections because, unlike wood, metals cannot be cut to a particular size or shaped easily.

Section	Available sizes	Section	Available sizes
Round rod 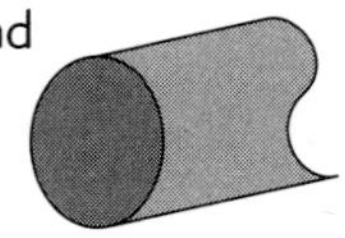	0, 3, 5, 6, 10, 12, 16, 20, 25, 32, 40, 50, 60	Sheet 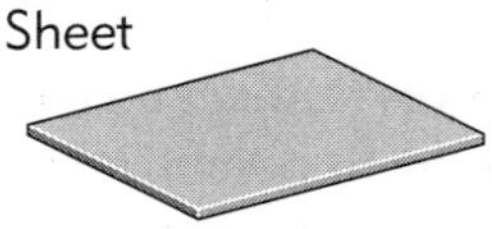	800 × 600 1200 × 600 1800 × 900 × 0.6 × 0.8 × 1 × 1.2 × 1.6 × 2.00
Square 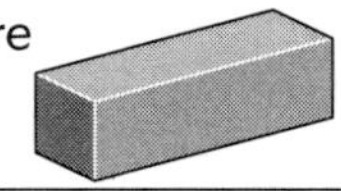	6, 8, 10, 12, 16, 20, 25	Round tube 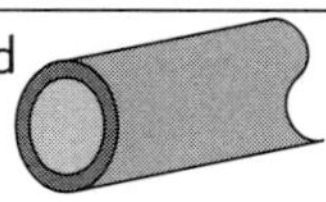	5, 6, 8, 10, 12, 16, 20, 25, 32, 40
Hexagonal 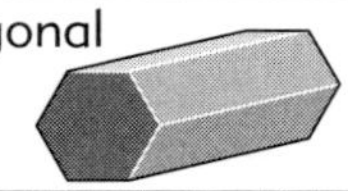	6, 8, 10, 12 16, 20, 25	Square tube 	12 × 12 16 × 16 20 × 20 25 × 25
Octagonal 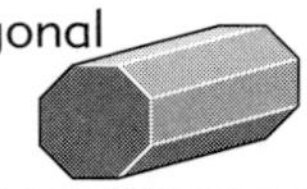	6, 8, 10, 12 16, 20, 25	Angle 	12 × 12 × 1.5 20 × 20 × 1.5 25 × 25 × 1.6
Flat strip 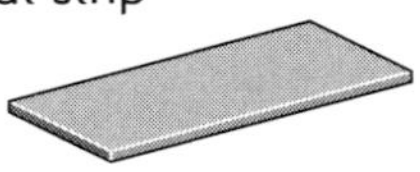	12 × 1.5 12 × 3 15 × 1.5 15 × 3 25 × 1.5 25 × 3 12 × 6 15 × 6 25 × 6	Channel 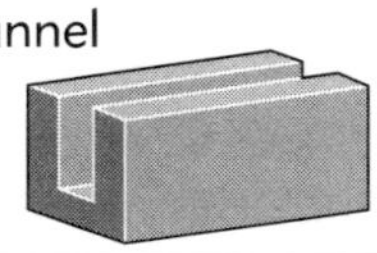	12 × 12 × 1.5 16 × 16 × 1.5

Common stock sizes.

Key word

Market form describes the range of shapes and sizes available.

Shaping and joining metal

Wasting

Examples of **wasting** include filing, sawing, cutting, drilling and machining.

Key word

Wasting is where the shape of the material is changed by cutting pieces off it.

Filing

Files are used to shape and smooth metal and plastic.

- *Crossfiling* – is a method of filing where the file is moved across the material using the full length of the file. It results in quick removal of waste but leaves a rough finish.
- *Drawfiling* – is used to produce a smooth finish, but removing less material, by moving the file sideways along the work.

There is a variety of different shaped files for specific purposes.

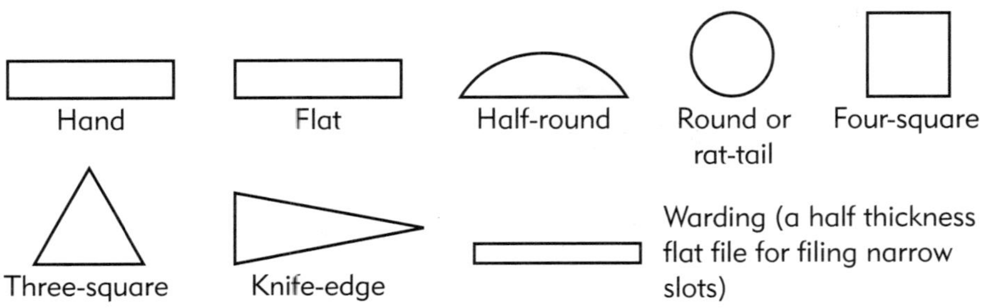

End views of files.

Note: The hand file has a safe edge – an edge without teeth that enables it to file into corners where the vertical surface must not be touched.

Sawing

- *Hacksaws* – are used for making straight cuts. The blade is held tightly in the frame with the teeth pointing forward.
- *Junior hacksaws* – are smaller versions and are used for lighter work.
- *Abrafile saws* – are circular blades with teeth that are used to cut curves in sheet material. The blade is held in a hacksaw frame.
- *Piercing saws* – are used to cut intricate curves in sheet metal. They have very thin blades held tightly in a frame. The teeth point backwards towards the handle so they cut when pulled towards you.

Cutting

- *Tin snips* – are used to cut sheet metal.
- *Straight snips* – are used for straight cuts and outside curves.
- *Curved snips* – are used for inside curves only.
- *Jewellers snips* – are available in straight and curved forms and are used for intricate work.

Drilling

Twist drills, made from high speed steel (HSS), are the most common drills used to drill holes. There are straight shank drills that fit into the chuck while morse taper shank drills fit directly into the drilling machine spindle. The twist part of the drill enables the 'swarf' (waste) to be removed.

Machining

Centre lathes are used to make or 'turn' cylindrical components in metal. They are also used to produce flat ends to lengths of round bars of metal and to drill holes in the ends of metal.

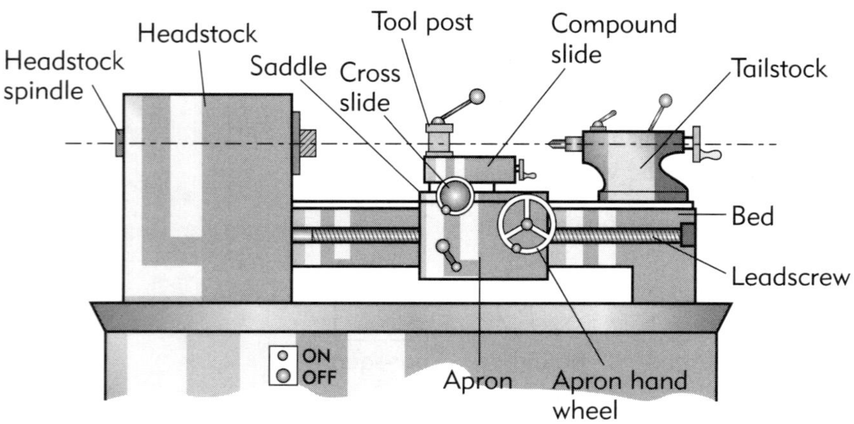

Parts of a lathe.

For most centre lathe operations, the work is held in a three-jaw self-centring chuck. Different sizes and types of metal may be held securely. There are two sets of jaws that enable large and small diameter material to be held and can be used to grip the inside of a hollow tube.

Centre lathe operations include the following:

- *Facing off* – describes the process by which a flat surface is produced, by turning, at the end of a length of cylindrical metal. The cutting tool moves across the end of the work at right angles to the axis of rotation of the work.

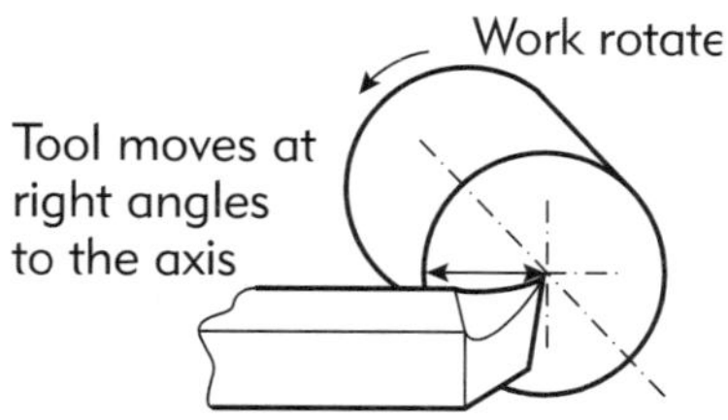

- *Parallel turning* – is the process by which metal is removed along the length of the metal, reducing the diameter of the metal. As the cutting tool moves sideways, parallel to the axis of rotation of the work, a cylindrical shape is produced.

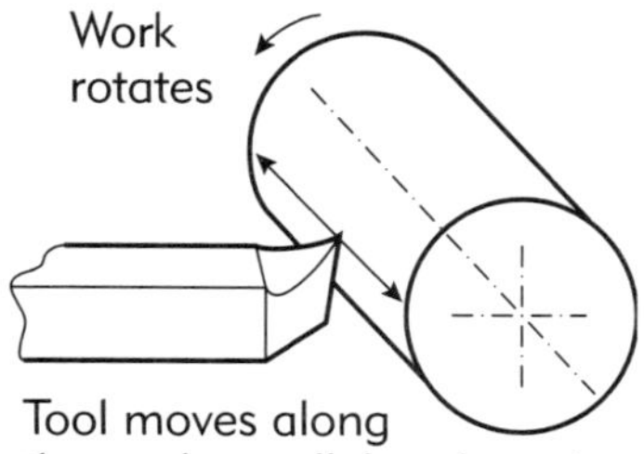

- *Centre drilling* – is the process by which holes may be drilled into the ends of cylindrical lengths of metal. It is more accurate than using a drilling machine because the metal is held in a chuck and the drill is held horizontally 'on centre' in the tailstock of the lathe.

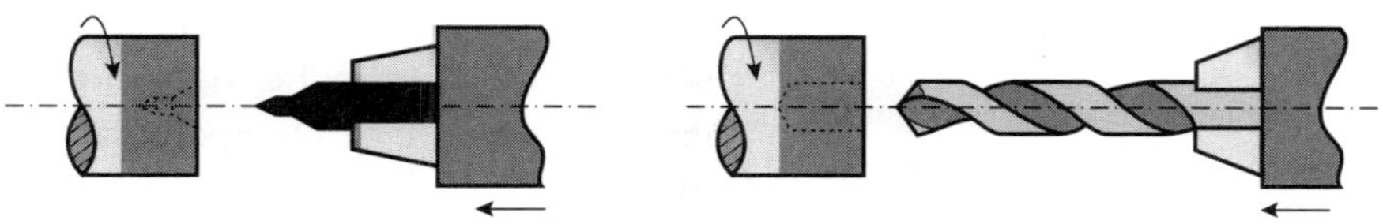

Centre drill compared to a twist drill.

Key word

Deforming means to change the shape of the material without affecting its state.

Deforming

An example of deforming is bending.

Bending

Sheet metal is held in folding bars to ensure that it is bent in a straight line. A small amount is bent at a time to prevent the metal from becoming stretched. In order to prevent the metal from being damaged, the metal is struck with either a hammer onto a hardwood block or by using a soft-faced hammer or mallet.

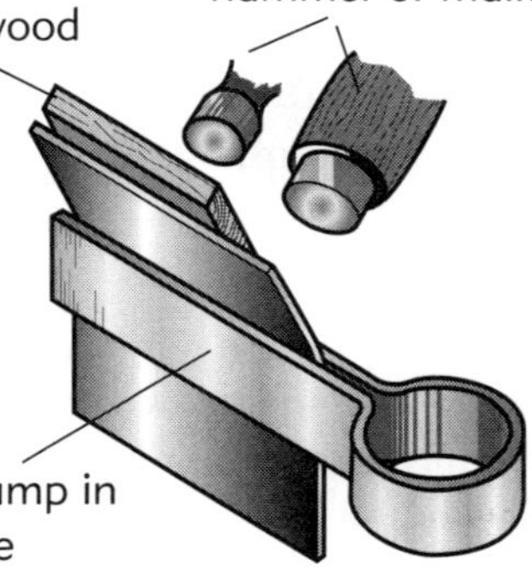

Bending metal.

Thin section metal in the form of 'rod' or 'flat' may be bent cold. Some metals would need to be annealed (softened) using heat before they can be bent to shape. When bending a number of pieces to an identical shape a simple jig would be used. The jig shown below is adjustable. The metal pegs can be removed and replaced in the required positions.

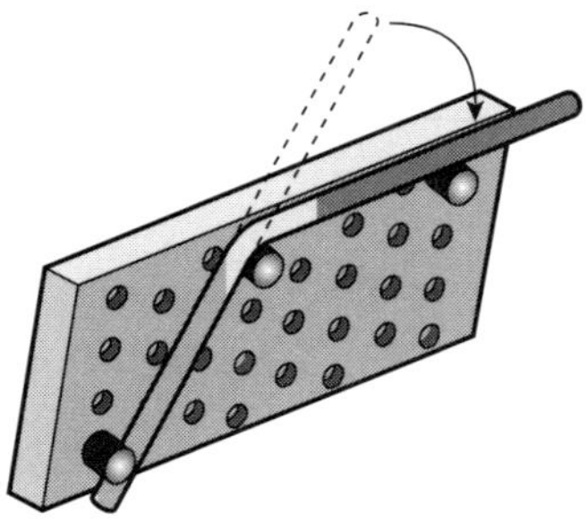

Bending metal using a jig.

Fabrication

Soldering

There are three types of **soldering**:

- Soft soldering is used to join electrical connections. The solder is an alloy of tin and lead with a low melting point.
- Silver or hard soldering is used in beaten or decorative metalwork. The solder is an alloy of copper and zinc with a small amount of silver added.
- Brazing is used to join mild steel. It uses a hard solder alloy of copper and zinc with a higher melting point than silver solder.

Stages in hard soldering or brazing a joint:

1 The surfaces to be joined must be clean. Use a file and emery cloth.
2 Make sure that the joint is a good fit.
3 Mix the correct flux and paint it onto the joint area. Also flux the end of the filler rod used to join the metals together. The flux is essential and has two purposes:
   - It keeps the joint clean by preventing oxidisation resulting from the heat of the flame.
   - It allows the melted solder or brazing rod to run into the joint.
4 Apply heat to the joint to dry the flux using a blow torch.
5 When the correct temperature is reached touch the joint with the filler rod. If it is hot enough, the rod will melt and run into the joint.
6 Remove the heat of the blow torch and allow the joint to cool.

Welding

Welding is a permanent method of joining metal together. It is where two pieces of metal (usually steel) are heated using a very hot oxy-acetylene flame or electric arc. When the applied heat melts the surfaces of the metal a filler rod is then melted into the joint to fill the gap between the pieces of metal. The joint should be as strong as the actual metal it has welded together.

Key words

Fabrication of metals refers to the ways in which they are joined either permanently or temporarily.

Soldering is a permanent method of joining metals together. The process uses an alloy that has a lower melting point than the metals being joined. When the joint is heated, the alloy melts and 'glues' the metals together.

There are two types of welding carried out in schools:

- oxy-acetylene gas welding
- electric arc welding, which uses an electric current to produce the necessary heat to fuse the metals together.

Pop riveting

Pop riveting is a permanent method of joining thin sheet metal or other thin materials. Holes are first drilled through the pieces to be joined. The hollow rivet is mounted on a head pin which is pushed into the rivet gun. The rivet is pushed into the pre-drilled holes and the gun is squeezed. This has the effect of pulling the pin through and expanding the rivet head. When the correct pressure is reached, the pin breaks off leaving the formed rivet with the pin head in it.

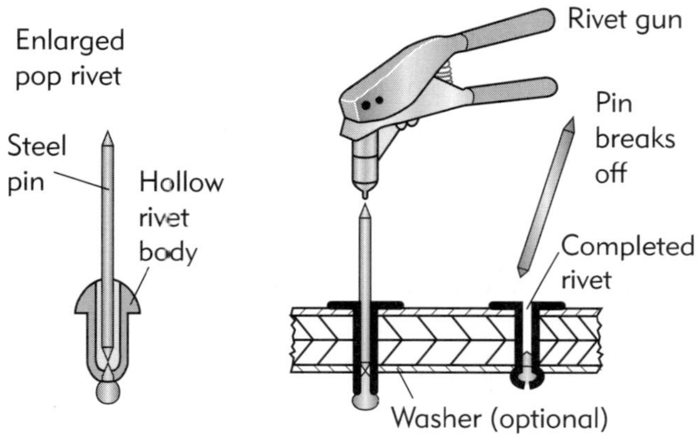

Pop riveting.

Machine screws, nuts and bolts

Machine screws, nuts and bolts are used as a simple semi-permanent method of fixing. They are useful where parts need to be taken apart for maintenance or repair.

- Machine screws are available in a wide range of materials, lengths, thread diameters and head shapes.
- Bolts have either a square or hexagonal head. They are ordered by the diameter of the thread and the length measured to the underside of the head. The thread may extend for all or part of the length.
- Nuts are either square or hexagonal for use with spanners, or wing nuts that can be removed by hand. Lock nuts are designed to withstand vibration.
- Washers are used to spread the load and protect the surface when the nut is tightened. Lock washers also prevent the nut from becoming loose due to vibration.
- Self-tapping screws are used to join sheet metal and plastic. They are made from hardened steel and as they are screwed into the material they cut their own thread. A pilot hole, the same diameter as the core of the screw, must be drilled first.

Reforming

Casting

There are different types of casting. Two methods are described below, one that can be carried out in school workshops (sand-casting) and an industrial method (die-casting).

Sand-casting – can be done in schools because it uses aluminium, which is relatively cheap, and a temperature of 750°C that can be achieved.

Stages in sand-casting:

1 Make a pattern from a close-grained hardwood.

2 The pattern is placed flat onto a moulding board and sprinkled with parting powder to help release from the sand later.

3 A 'drag' (bottom box) is placed over the pattern and finely sifted sand is packed around the pattern. Coarse sand is then rammed tightly into the drag until it is full. The surface is 'strickled off' flat using a metal strip.

4 The 'cope' (top box) is fitted on top of the drag. Sprue pins (wooden pegs) are positioned vertically inside the cope. (When removed later these will form the channels through which molten metal will run.) The cope is filled with tightly rammed sand.

5 The cope is then removed from the drag and the sprue pins withdrawn from the sand carefully. The resulting holes are known as the 'runner' and 'riser'.

6 The pattern is also withdrawn from the sand and 'gates' or channels connecting the runner and riser to and from the mould are cut into the sand.

7 The cope is then repositioned on top of the drag and the molten metal, heated in a crucible, is poured into the mould. The metal is poured down the runner, it flows into the mould and exits by way of the riser.

8 Allow the metal to cool, remove sand from around the solidified workpiece and remove completely from the sand.

9 Saw off excess metal and begin to clean up. This usually involves filing and machining.

Key word

Reforming is when the state of the material is changed from solid to liquid and then back to solid, for example casting and injection moulding.

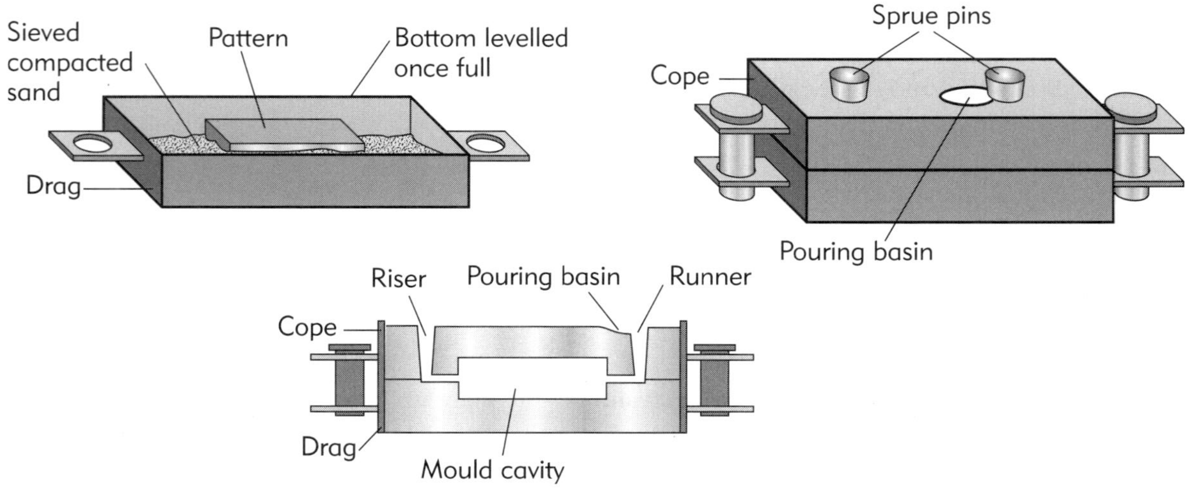

Stages in sand-casting.

Sand-casting is a slow, labour-intensive process suitable only for one-off production. Each time a casting is carried out the mould is destroyed. Therefore, when manufacturing in quantity, an alternative method such as die-casting is used.

In *die-casting* the mould or die is made from metal. It can be reused over and over again. The mould can be expensive to manufacture but costs are recovered because of the high numbers that can be manufactured using this process.

Pressure die-casting involves forcing the molten metal into the dies under hydraulic pressure. Metals cast in this way are usually low temperature alloys, and intricate shapes such as car cylinder heads can be manufactured.

Creating and processing materials to create more useful properties

Alloys are formed to create specific properties not present in a single metal. Examples of alloys are given in the tables of ferrous and non-ferrous metals on pages 45–6.

Annealing

Annealing is carried out in different ways depending on the metal to be worked:

- Steel is heated to bright red, allowed to soak, then left to cool slowly.
- Aluminium is covered with soap. The metal is heated and when the soap turns black this indicates that the required temperature is achieved and the metal is left to cool slowly.
- Copper is heated to cherry red. It can then be quenched in water.
- Brass is heated to dull red and allowed to cool slowly.

Key word

Annealing is the process whereby metal is made softer and easier to shape.

Hardening and tempering

Hardening is carried out on steel with a substantial carbon content. The more carbon, the harder the steel.

Steel is hardened by heating to cherry red, soaked at this temperature for a short time, then quenched vertically in oil, brine (salt water) or water. Quenching the metal horizontally can result in the metal cracking.

Hardening produces metal that is so brittle that it cannot be used. Therefore, this process is used alongside another process called **tempering** that makes the metal useable. The amount of hardness to be removed depends on what the metal product will be used for.

The steel is cleaned so that the different surface oxide or tempering colours can be seen clearly. As the steel is heated, it changes colour. When the required colour is visible on the steel it is immediately quenched in water. The following table gives details of some of the tempering colours and the uses for which the steel is used.

Key words

Hardening is done to increase the hardness and tensile strength of tool steel.

Tempering removes the extreme hardness and brittleness from the metal to make it tougher and more usable.

Tempering colours and uses of steel

Colour	Approximate temperature (°C)	Uses
Light straw	230	Lathe tools, scribers, dividers
Dark straw	245	Drills, taps and dies, punches
Brown	260	Plane blades, shears, lathe centres
Brown-purple	270	Knives, scissors, woodwork chisels
Purple	280	Cold chisels, axes, table knives
Blue	300	Springs, spanners, needles, screwdrivers

Preparing for manufacture and economic use of material

There is a wide range of standard sections because, unlike wood, metals cannot be cut and shaped to a particular size easily. Stock sizes are shown on page 47. Products made from metal should be fabricated using the standard or market forms available wherever possible.

Marking out tools

To measure and mark out a length of metal, use:

- a steel rule
- an engineers try square
- a scriber.

To mark a line parallel to a true edge, use:

- odd-leg calipers.

To mark out a circle or an arc, use:

- spring dividers – to make the mark on the metal
- a dot punch and hammer – to make an indentation into the surface for one of the legs of the dividers to locate.

To mark out the centre where a hole is to be drilled, use:

- a centre punch and hammer.

To mark out an irregular shape, use:

- templates made from paper or card glued onto the surface of the metal.

Finishing

Preparation and **finishing** of the metal is essential.

Steel may need to be:

- drawfiled, that is, filing along the length of the metal in one direction
- cleaned using different grades of emery cloth (an abrasive grit glued onto a cloth backing – grades range from fine to coarse).

Copper should be:

- pickled in an acid bath to remove grease and oxides
- washed in water before using steel wool or pumice powder to give a final clean.

Key word

Finishing is carried out in order to protect the metal from tarnishing and improve the appearance of the product.

Painting

1 Apply a primer to the bare metal. This helps the next coats of paint to adhere to the metal.

2 Apply an oil-based undercoat as the preparation for the final coat.

3 Apply a top coat, for example an oil-based gloss finish.

Paint can be applied by means of a brush or spray. Spray finishes give a more consistent, even finish but the paint needs to be applied in well-ventilated conditions.

A 'one-coat' paint, available in a smooth or hammered finish, gives a one-coat, quick-drying protective finish for ferrous metals without the need for a primer or undercoat.

Polishing

Polishing is carried out on metals such as stainless steel, copper or brass in order to show off the natural colour and lustre of the metal.

Polishing may be done by hand, using metal polish or by means of a polishing mop fitted onto a buffing machine. A polishing compound is applied to the mop and the workpiece held against the rotating mop. A high quality polished finish is possible if the appropriate preparation has been carried out.

In order to prevent the polished surface becoming tarnished, a clear cellulose lacquer may be applied by means of a brush or spray.

Dip coating

Coating with plastic is done to:

- protect the metal from corrosion
- provide electrical insulation
- enhance the appearance.

Products that are dip coated include refrigerator shelves, freezer baskets and handles for tools such as pliers.

In school workshops dip coating is carried out as follows:

1 Heat the metal to be coated in an oven to 180°C.

2 Plunge the metal into a tank of **fluidised** polythene powder for a few seconds.

3 Re-heat in the oven to produce a smooth, even finish.

4 Leave to cool.

> ***Key word***
>
> **Fluidisation** is where air is blown into the tank through the polythene powder so that when the metal is plunged into it, the powder will adhere to the surface of the metal forming an even coating.

Wood and wood-based materials

There are two 'families' of wood:

Hardwoods such as oak, ash and beech come from broad-leaved, deciduous trees, that is, trees that shed their leaves in autumn.

Softwoods such as pine come from coniferous (cone bearing) trees that remain evergreen all year round.

Common hardwoods

Tree	Source	Properties/working characteristics	Uses
Beech	Europe	Very tough, hard, straight and close-grained. Polishes well. Liable to warp	Chairs, floors, tools, turnery, toys, steam bent furniture
Ash	Europe	Wide-grained, tough, very flexible, finishes well	Tool handles, sports equipment including cricket stumps and hockey sticks, ladders
Elm	Europe	Tough, flexible, durable, water resistant, liable to warp	Garden furniture (treated), turnery, interior furniture
Oak	Europe	Heavy, hard, strong, tough, open-grain, finishes well	Boat building, floors, gate posts, high class furniture and fittings
Mahogany	Africa, South America	Easy to work, wide boards available, polishes quite well, interlocking grain	Indoor furniture, shop fittings, veneers
Teak	Burma, India	Hard, durable, natural oils resist moisture, fire, acids, alkalis. Straight grain, works well	Laboratory benches, high class furniture, veneers, garden furniture

Common softwoods

Tree	Source	Properties/working characteristics	Uses
Redwood (Scots Pine)	Northern Europe, Russia	Straight grain, knotty, easy to work, finishes well, durable	Most commonly used, construction work. Needs protection when used outdoors
Western Red Cedar	USA, Canada	Lightweight, knot-free, straight grain, contains natural oils that protect from weather, insects, rot	Outdoors, e.g. cladding of buildings, wall panelling
Parana Pine	South America	Hard, straight grain, almost knot-free, available in wide boards	Inside use only, e.g. staircases, built-in furniture
Whitewood (Spruce)	Northern Europe, Canada, USA	Fairly strong, resistant to splitting, easy to work	General indoor furniture

Market forms

Boards are 75 mm or more wide and less than 40 mm thick. Common thicknesses: 12, 16, 19, 22, 25 mm; common widths: 150–300 mm.
Planks are 40 mm or thicker.
Squares are square in section. Common sizes: 25 mm x 25 mm, 38 mm x 38 mm, 50 mm x 50 mm.
Strips are rectangular in section and less than 75 mm wide. Common sizes: 38 mm x 25 mm, 50 mm x 25 mm.

Manufactured boards

Advantages of manufactured boards

- Solid woods contain moisture and so they dry out and shrink. This can cause the wood to twist, warp and split. **Manufactured boards** are constructed in such a way as to solve this problem.
- Manufactured boards are available in larger sheet sizes, e.g. 2440 mm x 1220 mm, than wood cut directly from trees.
- Manufactured boards are more readily available from do-it-yourself centres and timber merchants than most hardwoods and softwoods.
- Manufactured boards tend to be less expensive than hardwoods and softwoods.

Disadvantages of manufactured boards

- The appearance of many boards is unattractive. When used to make household products they need to be faced with veneers or plastic coverings. The exposed edges of the boards need to lipped with a piece of solid wood or covered with veneer to hide their ugly appearance.
- Traditional wood constructions are generally not suitable with manufactured boards and new methods have been developed.

Key word

Manufactured boards are wood-based boards made by gluing together wood strips, veneers (thin layers of solid wood), fibre pulp or particles.

Commonly used manufactured boards

- Medium Density Fibreboard (MDF) – is made from tiny particles of wood and fibres compressed and glued together. It has no grain and a very smooth surface. It cuts and machines well. It can be painted or covered with veneers. It is used to make indoor furniture.
- Plywood – is made by 'laminating' or gluing together a number of veneers (plies). Each veneer is glued to the previous one with the grain running at 90°. This produces a very stable board that is unlikely to bend, twist or warp. To ensure that the grain of the top and bottom veneers of the plywood run in the same direction, there are always an odd number of veneers – 3, 5, 7, and so on. There are different grades of plywood for specific tasks: marine plywood for boat building; a cheap, coarse grade for concrete 'shuttering' in the building industry; and higher quality for doors and drawer bottoms in the furniture industry.
- Blockboard – is made by first gluing together softwood strips side by side and then sandwiching them between top and bottom veneers or plies. The grain of the plies runs at 90° to the softwood strips. Blockboard is used for furniture such as table tops.

- Chipboard – is made by compressing and gluing wooden chips together. Chipboard can be difficult to work and isn't very attractive. There are different grades for specific purposes, for example flooring quality or denser quality used for kitchen surfaces. When covered with tough veneer or plastic coating chipboard is attractive and sturdy.
- Hardboard – is made by compressing and gluing small wood fibres. One side of the board is usually smooth while the other has a rough texture. Hardboard is used for drawer bottoms and the backs of cabinets. When used for larger items, for example doors, it needs to be fixed to a wooden frame.

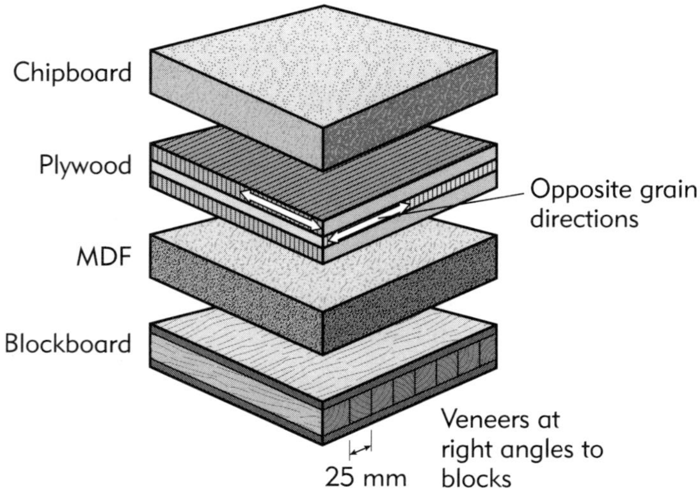

Commonly used manufactured boards.

Shaping and joining wood

Carcase constructions

- Corner joints used include butt and lapped butt (rebate).
- Shelves or partitions include housing joints.

a) Butt. b) Corner rebate or lap. c) Housing.

Stool constructions

Joints used include mortise and tenon, and dowel.

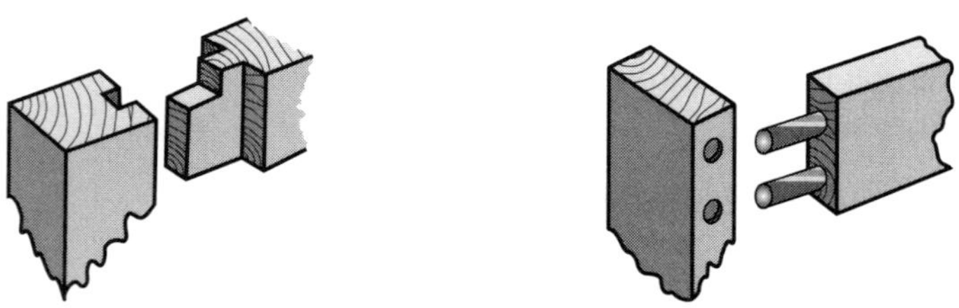

a) Mortise and tenon joint. b) Dowelled joint.

Key words

Carcase construction describes joints used in the construction of cabinets and boxes.

Stool construction describes those joints used to join together rails to legs in four-legged stools and tables.

Frame construction

Joints used include mortise and tenon, dowel, corner bridle and corner halving.

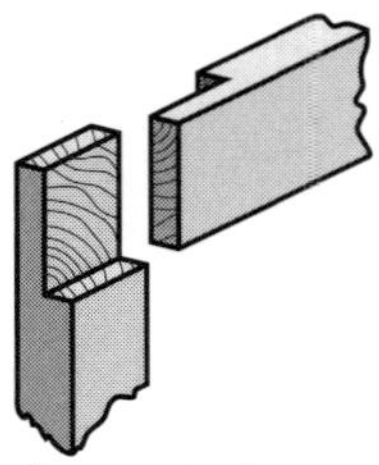

a) Corner halving.

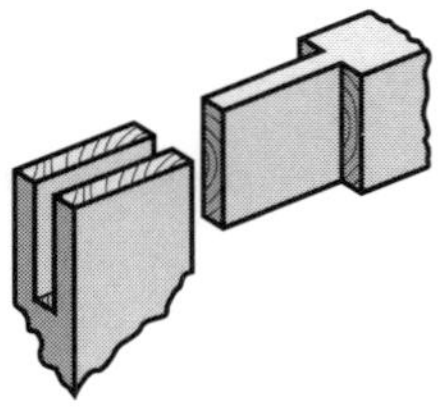

b) Corner bridle.

Where rails cross over each other, a cross halving joint may be used.

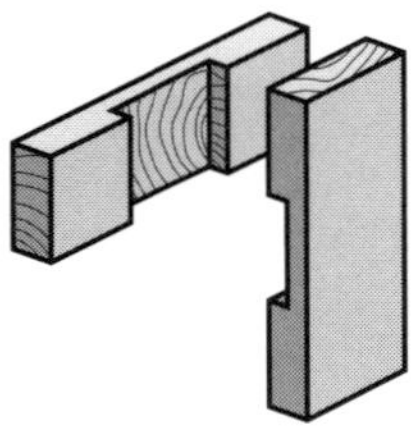

c) Cross halving.

Slab construction

Joints include butt (strengthened with corner blocks), corner rebate and knock-down (KD) fittings. (KD fittings are shown on page 60.)

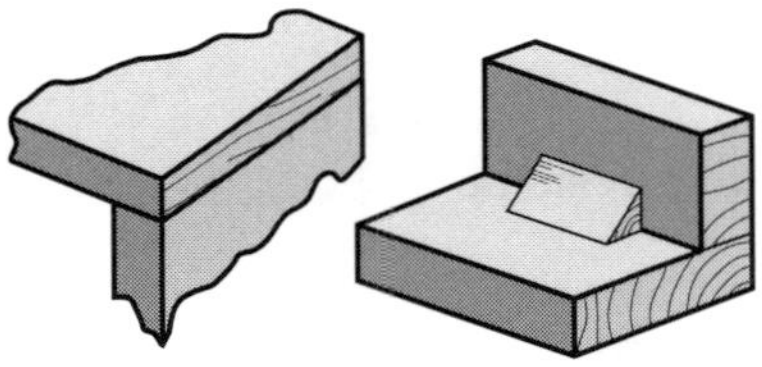

a) Butt with corner block.

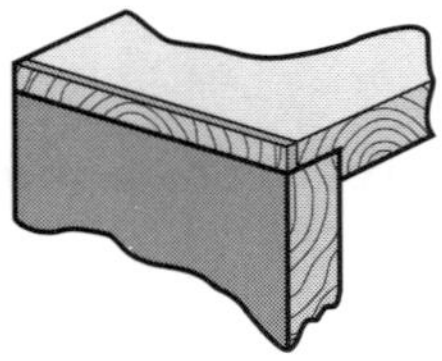

b) Corner rebate.

Adhesives

PVA adhesive

- Good general woodworking adhesive.
- Ready-mixed for ease of use.
- Water resistant varieties available.
- Takes 2–4 hours to set and requires pressure through clamping.
- Few health and safety problems.

Contact adhesive

- Used to glue plastic laminate to manufactured boards (suitable for large areas).
- Apply evenly to both surfaces to be glued.
- Leave until 'touch dry' (10–15 minutes).
- Position two surfaces accurately before applying final pressure to the two surfaces in contact. CAUTION: because most of these adhesives set when the surfaces come into contact with each other, accurate positioning is essential.

Key words

Frame construction describes those joints in the construction of frames used to strengthen doors or panels made from sheet material.

Slab construction describes those methods used to join together furniture made from sheets of manufactured board, for example the sides of a cabinet made from chipboard or plywood.

Synthetic resin adhesive

- Excellent woodworking adhesive, especially designed for boat building or any work in contact with water.
- White glue powder mixed with water to a creamy consistency.
- When mixed must be used within 30 minutes; wasteful if not used up.
- Apply to joints and cramp together under pressure and allow 6 hours to set.

Epoxy resin adhesive

- Used to glue together a variety of materials: wood, metal, some plastics, ceramics, glass.
- Two parts in two tubes: resin (glue) and hardener (catalyst).
- Two parts mixed in equal amounts.
- Pressure through clamping or weights is essential.
- Quick drying varieties will set in 3–4 hours. Heat makes the drying process quicker.

Fabrication: temporary joints

Screws

Types of screw used as a temporary method of fixing include:

- countersunk head screws – used where the head of a screw needs to be flush or slightly below the surface
- round head screws – used to fix hinges or brackets made from thin sheet metal to wood
- chipboard screws with a coarse thread – used for joining chipboard or other manufactured boards which tend to crumble when screwed with traditional screws.

Knock-down (KD) joints

- Plastic blocks are used for strengthening and joining a shelf to the side of a cabinet.
- Scan fittings are used to join legs and rails on a variety of small tables and television stands. Each joint has an Allen screw that screws into a threaded metal barrel.

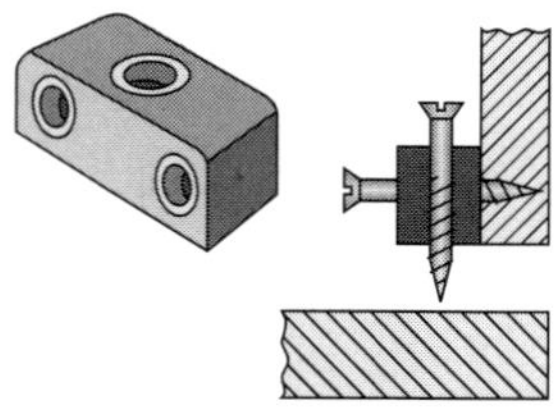

a) Plastic block.

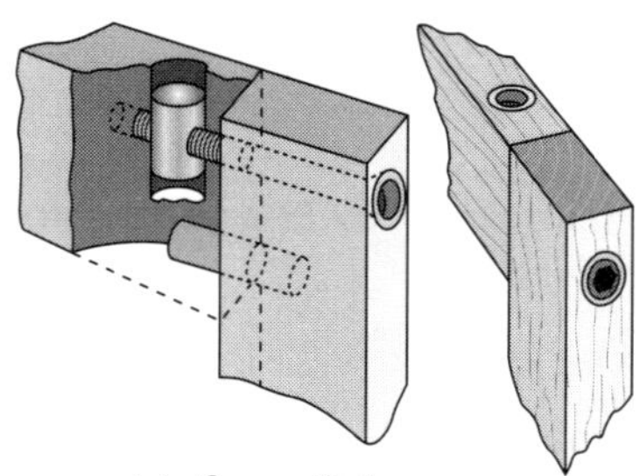

b) Scan fitting.

Nuts and bolts

Nuts and bolts are also a commonly used method of temporary fixing.

Material preparation

Material preparation includes marking out, sawing, planing and end-sanding.

- Marking out and sawing a piece of wood to the correct length. Tools required: steel rule, try square, pencil or marking knife.
- Marking out and planing to width. Tools required: marking gauge set to the required width, jack plane for quick removal of waste wood.
- Checking for flatness. Place the edge of a steel rule on the edge or surface to be tested and hold up to the light. If the wood is flat, then little or no light will be seen under the steel rule. If you can see light, then the wood will need to be planed.
- Checking for squareness. Place the stock of the try square up against the side or edge of the wood and hold up to the light. If the wood is square, then little or no light will be seen under the blade of the try square. If you see light, then the wood will need to be planed.
- Squaring the ends. Planing end grain on narrow pieces of wood can be difficult and the end grain can split. The end grain can be squared quickly and accurately by placing the wood against a sanding disc and checking with a try square.

Key word

Material preparation describes the processes involved in getting pieces of wood to the correct size and shape ready for manufacture.

Sawing

Most operations can be carried out using four saws.

- Tenon saw – used for making accurate straight saw cuts across or along the grain of the wood. The depth of cut is limited by the 'back' of the saw.
- Coping saw – used for cutting curves in thin wood or manufactured boards.
- Scroll saw – an electric saw with a blade that reciprocates (goes up and down) used to cut curved or straight shapes in wood. Blades are thin and care must be taken not to force the blade too quickly when cutting. Some scroll saws take blades that can saw plastic and thin sheet metal.
- Jig saw – used for similar operations to the scroll saw but whereas the scroll saw is stationery and the wood moved about the blade, the electric jig saw is hand-held and is moved around the shape to be cut.

Cutting

Planes are used to clean up and prepare wood to the correct size:

- Jack plane – used for quick removal of waste wood when planing to size. The plane has a long sole that makes it well suited to making wood flat.
- Smoothing plane – shorter than the jack plane, used for finishing, e.g. cleaning up the outside of a box that has been glued ready for fine finishing.

Special planes are used for specific purposes:

- Plough plane – used to cut out grooves along the grain.
- Rebate plane – used for cutting rebates into the edge or side of a piece of wood.
- Router plane – used to level the bottom of housings across the grain.
- Block plane – used for small work such as planing end grain on small pieces of wood.

Chisels are used for shaping or cutting wood where planes cannot be used:

- Firmer chisel – a general purpose chisel that can, with care, be used with a mallet.
- Bevel-edge chisel – used to get into corners smaller than 90 degrees, e.g. dovetail joints. Because the edges have been ground to a bevel they are not as robust as the firmer chisel.
- Mortise chisel – used with a mallet to cut out mortises (square or rectangular holes in wood). They are designed to withstand heavy duty use.

Surform tools and power routers

Surform tools are used to shape wood. The blades cut with an action similar to that of a cheese grater. There are a variety of shaped blades including flat, half-round and round. When blunt, blades can be replaced quickly.

Power routers are used to cut out grooves, rebates, chamfers and mouldings. There are different shaped cutters for different purposes available in different diameter sizes. The router is hand-held and is moved along or across the work as the cutter rotates.

Drilling

- Twist drills – see page 48.
- Countersink drills – used to produce a countersink in wood, metal or plastic so that screw heads are flush or slightly below the surface of the material.
- Flat bits – used in electric drills to drill quickly and accurately without having to apply a great deal of pressure. Available in a range of sizes from 6 mm to 40 mm diameter. Flat bits have a point that must first be located on the surface of the wood.
- Saw tooth bits – used in electric drills, are used to drill smooth-sided, flat-bottomed holes. The saw tooth cutting action allows for quick and efficient removal of waste. Available in a range of sizes: 10–50 mm diameter.

Sanding

Machine sanding uses different grades of abrasive paper depending on the material and process being carried out.

- Sanding discs are useful for squaring up end grain on lengths of wood or for completing convex (outside) shapes.
- Orbital sanders are hand held and are used for fine finishing. They can sand down small or large areas such as a table top that would take too long by traditional hand methods.
- Belt sanders use a continuous abrasive belt held between front and back rollers. They tend to be quite fierce and need more control than orbital sanders.

Machining

Power routers are used to cut grooves, rebates, chamfers and mouldings (explained above).

Finishing

Preparing the wood (cleaning up) before applying a finish.

1. Use a smoothing plane to produce a smooth, clean surface.
2. Use a medium grade of glasspaper wrapped around a cork block to sand down along the grain of the wood.
3. Wipe the surface clean to remove dust.
4. Repeat stages 2 and 3 using progressively finer grades of glasspaper.

Key word

Finishing is carried out in order to:

- protect the wood from weathering and decay
- protect the wood from minor scratches
- improve the appearance of the product.

Painting

1 Apply a primer to seal the surface of bare wood.
2 Apply an undercoat.
3 Rub down surface with very fine grade of glasspaper, e.g. 'Flour' or '00'.
4 Apply a final coat, e.g. an oil-based or acrylic gloss finish.

Types of applied finish

Paint is available in many forms:

- Emulsion paint is suitable for covering large areas because it is relatively inexpensive and can be applied with a large brush or roller. It is water-based and is not very durable.
- Oil-based paint, including non-drip types, is durable and weatherproof.
- Acrylic paint is quick drying, waterproof and has a denser colour.

Varnish gives a clear, tough, durable finish and is available in different finishes: gloss (shiny), satin (slightly shiny) and matt (dull). Coloured varnishes are used to give wood a combined varnish and colour in a single coat. A good varnished finish depends on the careful application of several coats that are allowed to dry and sanded down with fine glasspaper between each coat.

Clear polishes allow the natural beauty of the grain to show through:

- French polish is a mixture of shellac and methylated spirits and is applied by means of a cloth rubber. Similar to French polish are 'White' polish and 'Button' polish. As with most finishes, the final quality depends on the careful build-up of separate layers and sanding down between coats.
- Wax polish can be applied on top of French polish or wood first sealed with cellulose. Different types of wax including beeswax or silicone may be applied.
- Stains do not protect the wood but are used to show off the grain and give the wood the appearance of a different, more expensive wood. Brightly coloured stains can be used to produce attractive finishes on products such as toys.
- Waterproof preservatives protect by penetrating deeply into the wood rather than simply coating the surface like varnish. Wood used outdoors may suffer attack from fungus, insects or the weather. Creosote is a cheap oil-based preservative that is easy to apply to garden sheds and fences. More expensive preservatives work more effectively than creosote and have a better appearance. There are several brands of preservative on the market, many of which are available in different colours.

Plastics and composites

There are two 'families' of plastics:

- Thermoplastics such as polythene and acrylic can be heated to make them soft so that they can be shaped or formed. When cool they return to their rigid form. This process may be repeated many times.
- Thermosetting plastics such as melamine can also be heated to make them soft to form and shape, but this process can only be carried out once.

Common thermoplastics

Common name	Properties/working characteristics	Uses
Low density polythene	Range of colours, tough, good electrical insulator and chemical resistance	Washing-up liquid and detergent bottles, bin liners, carrier bags
High density polythene	Range of colours, hard, stiff, good chemical resistance, high impact	Milk crates, bottles, pipes, buckets, bowls
Polystyrene	Range of colours, stiff, hard	Disposable cups, fridge linings, model kits, food containers
Expanded polystyrene	Lightweight, absorbs shock, good sound and heat insulator	Sound and heat insulation, protective packaging
Polypropylene	Hard and lightweight, good chemical resistance, can be sterilised, good impact	Medical equipment, syringes, crates, string, rope, chair shells, containers with integral (built in) hinges.
Nylon	Hard, tough, self-lubricating, resistant to chemicals and high temperatures	Gear wheels, bearings, curtain rail fittings, clothing, combs, power tool cases
Acrylic	Stiff, hard, clear, durable outdoors, easily machined and polished, good range of colours, excellent impact resistance (glass substitute)	Illuminated signs, aircraft canopies, car rear light clusters, baths, Perspex sheet
ABS	Tough, high impact strength, lightweight, scratch resistant, chemical resistance, excellent appearance.	Kitchenware, safety helmets, car parts, telephones, food mixers

Common thermosetting plastics

Common name	Properties/working characteristics	Uses
Urea-formaldehyde	Stiff, hard, brittle, heat resistant, electrical insulator, range of colours	White electrical fittings, domestic appliance parts, wood glue
Melamine-formaldehyde	Stiff, hard, strong, range of colours, scratch and stain resistant	Tableware, decorative laminates, electrical insulation
Phenol-formaldehyde	Stiff, hard, strong, brittle, heat resistant	Dark electrical fittings, saucepan handles

Common thermosetting plastics (continued)

Common name	Properties/working characteristics	Uses
Epoxy resin	Resistant to chemicals and wear, very strong when reinforced.	Araldite™ adhesive mixed with a hardener
Polyester resin	Brittle on its own but very strong when laminated with glass fibre, good electrical insulator	Glass fibre boats, chair shells

Market forms

Many plastics such as polythene are available as powder or granules while the most commonly used, including acrylic, are available as sheet, rod and tube.

Examples of **composites** include the following:

- Glass reinforced plastic (GRP) where glass-fibre mat is impregnated with polyester resin to form a waterproof product. Canoes, surfboards and Lotus three-wheel cars are made from GRP.
- Carbon fibre (graphite) in the form of thread, rope or cloth is cast with a thermosetting plastic and moulded to shape. Some cycle frames, fishing rods and golf clubs are made from carbon fibre.

Because different products require different properties, substances are added to the raw material in order to achieve these properties. For example, to make some plastics very soft and pliable, 'plasticisers' are added; dyes and pigments may be added to produce a particular colour; to increase the 'bulk' of a product cheaply, fillers are added.

> ***Key word***
>
> **Composites** are the result of combining two or more materials. The composite material has the advantage of possessing the characteristics of both materials.

Shaping and joining plastics

Many of the tools used when working with wood and metal can be used with plastics.

Material preparation

Most of the tools used for marking out metal are appropriate for plastics (see page 54).

Most of the tools used in the preparation of wood to width and length are appropriate for plastics (see page 61).

- Scribers make a permanent mark that could damage work if mistakes are made. A felt marker pen or a 'chinagraph' (soft wax) pencil can give an accurate mark that can be erased later.
- Marking gauges are suitable tools to mark the width of a piece of wood but odd-leg calipers, used with metal, are more appropriate when marking out plastics.

Filing
The same files and filing techniques that are used with metal can be applied to plastics. Care has to be taken to keep the files clean as soft plastics can easily clog the file teeth. For information about files and filing, see page 47.

Sawing
Many of the saws used to cut metal and wood can also be used with plastic. For information about the hacksaw, abrafile and piercing saw, see page 48, and for information about the tenon, coping and scroll saw, see page 61.

Cutting
Some of the planes used to shape and clean up wood may be used with acrylic plastic. For information about planes, see page 61.

Drilling
For information about twist drills, see page 48, and for information about saw tooth bits and countersink drills, see page 62.

Machining
The centre lathe processes described on pages 48–9 apply also to the machining of plastics.

Fabrication

The most commonly used plastic in school workshops is acrylic sheet.

Temporary fixing may be carried out using any of the nuts, bolts and screws described on page 60. Permanent methods of joining acrylic can be done using a solvent such as Tensol cement. There are strict safety rules when using this solvent:

- You must be in a well-ventilated area.
- Do not inhale the fumes.
- Prevent contact with eyes and skin.

Tensol cement works well when there is sufficient surface area to be joined together. Edge joining is difficult and unsuitable. Tensol cement requires some pressure from a vice, clamps or weights to allow it to set. Under normal workshop conditions, joints will set within 15 minutes.

Deforming plastic
The processes of bending, vacuum forming and press moulding are described on pages 21–2.

Laminating *glass reinforced plastic (GRP)*
The quality of the final product depends upon the quality of the mould. Since the glass-fibre mat is laid onto the mould, the surface in contact will be smooth. Products made from GRP include boat hulls.

> ***Key word***
>
> **Laminating** is the process whereby two or more layers of material are bonded together to form a thicker single layer.

Stages in the making of a product using GRP:

1 Apply a silicon-free wax and release agent to the surface of the mould onto which the fibre glass will be laid up.
2 Apply a gel-coat resin, with pigment added to give the required colour to the mould.
3 When dry, lay glass-fibre mat onto the gel-coat.
4 Apply polyester resin onto the mat and 'stipple' (impregnate) the resin into the mat to seal it.
5 Repeat stages 2 and 3 depending on how many layers are required. Canoes, for example, may have only two or three layers.
6 When the mat and resin have 'cured' (hardened) the glass fibre product can be removed from the mould.

Moulds are re-usable.

A catalyst is added to the gel-coat and polyester resin before application to produce a chemical action that makes the resin set hard.

Reforming plastic

Injection moulding

This is the most commonly used plastics-manufacturing process and is used to make precision items for cameras, printers, and so on, as well as larger scale products such as garden tables and chairs.

The process involves:

1 feeding granules of plastic into a hopper
2 heating the granules to create a 'plastic', not liquid, state
3 forcing or injecting the plastic into a mould.

The cost of the 'tool' or mould is high so this process is only suitable for high volume long runs. The principles of injection moulding can be seen when using a hot melt glue gun.

Extrusion

Extrusion is similar to injection moulding except that the heated plastic is forced through the 'die' by means of a rotating screw. The shape of the die will produce the shape of the product being extruded. Products made using this process include curtain rails, drainpipes and guttering.

> ***Key word***
>
> **Extrusion** can be thought of as a process like squeezing toothpaste through the end of a tube.

Fine finishing and polishing plastics

The most commonly used plastic in school workshops is acrylic sheet. The surface of acrylic plastic is excellent, highly polished and shiny. Edges of the plastic become rough and scratched as a result of sawing, sanding and filing. In order to achieve the same quality of finish as the surface, you should carry out the following:

1 Remove deep scratches by means of drawfiling or a scraper. (Scrapers can be made from hacksaw blades.)
2 Rub the edges on silicon carbide (wet or dry) paper. Use a medium/ coarse grit 150.
3 Repeat the process using a finer grit 400.
4 Apply an appropriate polishing compound, such as Vonax, to a soft calico mop and apply the edge of the plastic to it to produce a high quality finish.

'Smart' and modern materials

Shape memory alloy (SMA)

Nitinol is an example of a shape memory alloy (SMA). It is made from a mixture of nickel and titanium and is available in many shapes or sections but is commonly used as wire. It is used to produce mechanical movement.

SMA works by 'remembering' a shape when heated to a specific temperature. At room temperature the SMA wire can be reshaped but when reheated to the original temperature, known as the transition temperature, the wire will return to its original shape. SMA can be used to move parts of robots, open or close a bolt, or raise or lower a valve.

Polymorph

Polymorph is a type of plastic available in granule form. The granules become soft when immersed in hot water. The plastic may then be moulded by hand to the required shape. By re-immersing the plastic in hot water it can be remoulded. At room temperature polymorph can be machined and cut in the same way as other plastics.

Polymorph is excellent for handles of tools as it can be ergonomically shaped and, since it shrinks as it cools, there is no need to glue it onto the tool itself.

Three examples of modern materials

- Carbon fibre (graphite) is a composite material that combines great strength with a light weight to produce a material capable of outperforming most metal alloys (see also page 45).
- Kevlar is also a composite material and is a fibre impregnated with resin. It is used to produce canoes, bullet-proof vests and helmets. It has the same properties as carbon fibre.
- Plastazote is a high quality closed cell polyethelene foam that can be used in direct contact with the skin. It is frequently used as protective packaging and, in tube form, can be slipped over handles of household utensils and cutlery to give better grip.

Using pre-manufactured standard components

Pre-manufactured components are those items that are bought (often from do-it-yourself stores) and then used in the manufacture of products or as products themselves. The vast majority of components used are made from metal.

Manufacturers keep costs down by using only standard sizes, so reducing the amount of stock they need to carry.

The main advantage of using pre-manufactured components is that they are available in a range of standard sizes. It is cheaper to buy pre-manufactured standard components than making them yourself.

Key word

'Smart' materials react to environmental changes such as temperature or light and appear to act intelligently. For example, the lenses in some sunglasses react to changing light conditions by darkening in bright sunlight.

Examples of pre-manufactured standard components

Metal components

- Screws, nuts and bolts.
- Nails and pins.
- Cup hooks and eyes.
- Hinges.
- Brackets and shelving systems.
- Locks and catches.
- Door furniture (letterplates, handles, bolts, locks).
- Knock-down (KD) fittings; some of which are plastic.

Wooden components

- Dowel and mouldings (shaped lengths of wood used for finishing the edges of a piece of furniture or for picture frames).
- Solid wooden wheels.
- Handles and knobs (also made from plastic).
- Pre-glued, iron-on veneers.
- Solid wood and Contiboard (manufactured board) shelving in standard lengths and widths with a finished edge.
- Solid wood brackets for shelving systems.

Plastic components

- Rawlplugs used when screwing into cement or concrete.
- Cups and caps used with screws.
- Studs used as supports for CDs.

Effects of pollution, waste and recyclability on society

Manufacturing industry

The manufacturing industry:

- uses some resources that cannot be renewed including fossil fuels
- adds to the 'greenhouse effect' (global warming) by burning large quantities of fossil fuels, that is, oil, coal and gas
- creates waste that has to be disposed of.

To find out how environmentally friendly a product is, a cradle-to-grave (life-cycle analysis) can be carried out. This examines the raw materials used, the manufacturing processes involved, the product in use, possible recycling and final disposal.

Consumer demands

Over the past 50 years, demands for consumer goods have increased dramatically. Some products are made to last while others are designed to last only for a short time. Some products are designed so that when one component breaks down the whole product is thrown away because it is uneconomical to repair. Some products are designed to wear out quickly, others have a limited life because they reflect a particular fashion. From the consumers' viewpoint, this can be expensive; in terms of the environment, it is very wasteful. For the manufacturer, it means jobs for employees and profits from increased sales.

Waste

Most solid waste is disposed of through landfill or incineration. Landfill gases are given off into the atmosphere and add to global warming. Incineration creates gas emissions that have to be controlled. Industries have to meet high standards when dealing with these pollutants.

Chemical waste is sometimes disposed of into rivers. Only certain levels are permitted but monitoring these can be difficult.

To minimise the damage to the environment, manufacturers need to:

- reduce the amount of material used in the manufacture of the product
- reduce the energy used during manufacture by increasing efficiency levels
- reduce the amount of packaging used to protect products
- make the product from recycled materials
- re-use those parts of products that can be saved when the product is disposed of.

Recycling waste materials and waste energy is essential for the future of the planet.

Recycling:

- saves non-renewable resources
- reduces energy consumption and gas emissions that damage the atmosphere
- helps to control pollution linked to the manufacturing and disposal processes
- reduces the dependence on raw materials.

Key points

You must be able to:

- explain the specific properties of materials
- name a suitable specific material (wood/metal/plastic) for a particular purpose
- describe a property required by a particular material
- describe the market forms available for wood, metal and plastic
- explain different ways of shaping and joining materials and name the tools and equipment needed to carry out such operations
- give examples of materials that are produced as a result of being combined and processed
- explain how materials are prepared economically for manufacture
- explain how materials are 'finished' and name finishes for specific purposes
- identify pre-manufactured standard components that could be used when manufacturing
- explain the effects of pollution, waste and recyclability on society.

Questions

1 a Name a suitable material from which aircraft parts could be made.
  b Describe one property of the material that makes it suitable.

2 Explain why you might need to anneal a piece of metal.

3 Explain the properties of teak that make it particularly good for making garden furniture.

4 State two advantages of using manufactured boards.

5 Describe where you might use each of the following constructions in wood:
  a lapped butt joint
  b mortise and tenon joint
  c housing joint

6 State two reasons for applying a finish to a product made from wood or metal.

7 Name two plastics products that are manufactured using extrusion.

8 Name two 'smart' materials and explain why they could be considered to be 'intelligent'.

9 State two advantages to society of recycling materials.

Activities

1 a Select three products made from different materials – wood, metal and plastic – that might be found in a kitchen.
  b Explain what special properties each material has in order to carry out its purpose.

2 Complete the table below by naming some of the different products in your home, the type of finish and the method of application.

Product	Type of finish	Method of application

3 Draw an item of furniture used in a bedroom or study:
  a Name the materials used.
  b Identify the construction or manufacturing processes used.
  c Name any pre-manufactured standard components used.

Systems and control

This section will cover:

- The three parts of a system.
- Use of sub-systems to control production processes.
- Importance of 'feedback' to a system.
- Feedback to control your own batch production system.
- Mechanisms and motion.

Systems, sub-systems and control

The operations or activities within a **system** may be mechanical, electronic, structural or pneumatic. In this exam you will be asked specific questions about mechanical systems and only need to be aware of the other types.

Think of a bicycle as a mechanical system which is made up of several **sub-systems** such as the frame, brakes, wheels and gears and pedals.

When riding a bicycle the cyclist provides the **control**. For example, the speed and acceleration is controlled by means of the pedals, chain and sprockets and a gear system. The steering is controlled by means of the handlebars, and slowing down is controlled by means of a braking system.

Three parts of a system

Every system has three parts to it:

input → process → output.

When riding a bicycle the **input** would be the energy produced by the cyclist in order to make the pedals turn.

When riding a bicycle the **process** involves the energy you put into pedalling and how this is converted into moving the chain and connecting sprockets in order to make the wheels move.

Hopefully, when you pedal the bicycle its wheels turn making the bicycle move forward. This is the **output**.

Use of sub-systems to control production processes

Consider two production process systems carried out in school workshops:

- drilling machine
- vacuum forming machine.

Drilling machine

- *Input:* switch on drilling machine.
- *Process:* switch starts motor → pulley wheels rotate → belt transmits movement from rear pulley wheel to front pulley wheel ('driver' to 'driven') → drill chuck rotates → apply pressure to handle of drilling machine to bring drill in contact with workpiece.
- *Output:* drills hole in workpiece.

Key words

Systems are a series of components, operations or activities that, when joined together, enable a specific task to be carried out.

Sub-systems are the individual parts of a system.

Control is the way by which the system is managed.

Input is what goes into the system to start it.

Process is a series of operations which converts (changes) energy, materials or movement to produce the desired effect.

Output is the outcome or the actual desired effect.

Sub-systems used in this production process include:

- on-off switch
- electric motor
- pulley system
- chuck fitted into machine spindle
- drill tightened in chuck
- drill table set at correct height
- spring-return handle
- depth gauge.

Control is achieved by means of:

- altering the speed by repositioning the belt connecting the pulley wheels (remember the general rule: large drill = slow speed; small drill = faster speed)
- setting the position of the table at the correct height
- setting the required depth of the drill bit by means of a depth gauge
- applying the required amount of pressure on the drill bit depending on its speed and diameter and the type of material being drilled.

Vacuum forming machine

- *Input:* switch on machine.
- *Process:* position mould on platen → lower platen → clamp plastic sheet in place → move heater over plastic sheet → wait until plastic becomes soft → remove heater → raise mould on platen → turn on pump to suck out air.
- *Output:* plastic sheet is formed to shape.

Sub-systems used in this production process include:

- on-off switch
- lever-operated platen (table on which the mould is positioned)
- toggle clamps (to create an airtight seal)
- electric heater
- electric pump
- mould or former.

Control is achieved by means of:

- heater controls used to set specific zones (inside or outside areas of the heating element)
- heater settings ranging from minimum to maximum heat
- time that the heat is applied to the sheet plastic (dependent on the type and thickness of the plastic and the shape and size of the mould or former).

Importance of 'feedback' to a system

When considering how effective a bicycle is working as a system, for example, the cyclist would be aware of its performance. The ride could be excellent in terms of braking, balance, road holding and cornering, and so on, but it could be that acceleration is poor because the gears do not engage correctly or quickly enough, or that braking was slow, sluggish and potentially dangerous due to incorrect adjustment of the brake levers or worn brake blocks. These effects give immediate **feedback** to the cyclist.

Key word

Feedback is the way that information is passed back from a later part of a system to an earlier part. The information tells you how well the system is working.

Feedback to control your own batch production system

When you designed a product for your internally assessed coursework project you were required to design a control system to enable your product to be manufactured as the first of a batch of 50 identical products. You are likely to have used a jig, former, template, mould or computer system. Feedback will help you to assess the effectiveness of the performance of your control system.

To continue with the example of a drilling machine as a system used to control production processes (see pages 72–3), let's now consider the type of feedback you could obtain from using a drilling jig. A drilling jig used to drill holes in strips of wood of a specific size was discussed on page 20 and its 'plus points' noted. However, as a control system, feedback from use would indicate some drawbacks in the system:

- The jig allows holes to be drilled at a 'set' distance from the end of each strip without the need to mark out the positions for the holes. However, when holes are to be drilled along the length of the strips and they are then inserted into the sides of the jig, marking out is essential. Because this means that each hole has to be aligned with the drill it is unlikely that the holes will be in identical positions and it also slows down the process.
- This jig does not allow for short lengths to be used since they would be difficult to hold securely or safely.
- This jig does not allow for variations in width or thickness of the strips to be drilled.

Mechanisms and motion

Key word

The purpose of a **mechanism** is to transform (change) an input motion and force into the required output motion and force. (The terms 'input' and 'output' have been described earlier in the section.)

There are four types of motion used in **mechanical** systems. The arrows are the symbols that show the type of motion.

- Linear – when an object moves in a straight line such as a car moving along the road.
- Reciprocating – when an object moves backwards and forwards such as a saw cutting through a piece of wood. It also applies to objects that move up and down such as a sewing machine needle.
- Rotary – when an object moves in a circular manner such as the hands of a clock or a wheel of a car.
- Oscillating – when an object moves along a curved path such as a swing or pendulum of a clock.

a) Linear. b) Reciprocating. c) Rotary. d) Oscillating.

Mechanisms can also be used to do the following:

- Change the type of movement, e.g. a scroll saw with an electric motor providing rotary input movement but a blade that has reciprocating output.
- Change the direction of motion, e.g. pulling the cord on window blind downwards makes the blind move upwards – the pulley system at the top provides the change of direction.
- Change an axis of rotation, e.g. when you turn the handle of a food whisk (rotary movement), the beaters of the whisk also rotate, but the bevel gear mechanism has changed the rotation from a vertical plane into a horizontal plane.
- Transmit movement and force, e.g. how the movement from the pedals of a bicycle is transmitted (passed on) to the rear wheel.

Gears

Simple gear trains

When **gearing down**, the output shaft rotates more slowly than the input shaft but with more force. In the example below, because there are three times as many teeth on the output gear as on the input gear, the input shaft has to rotate three times to make the output shaft rotate once. The output shaft turns at one-third the speed of the input shaft, but with greater force. Gear ratio is calculated by:

$$\frac{\text{Number of teeth on driver gear}}{\text{Number of teeth on driven gear}} = \frac{15}{45} = \frac{1}{3}$$

Gear ratio is written as 3:1 because it takes 3 turns of the driver to 1 turn of the driven.

When **gearing up**, the output shaft will rotate faster than the input shaft but with less force. In the example below, because there are three times as many teeth on the input gear as on the output gear, the input shaft has to rotate only once while the output shaft rotates three times. The output shaft rotates three times as fast as the input shaft but with less force. Gear ratio is calculated by:

$$\frac{\text{Number of teeth on driver gear}}{\text{Number of teeth on driven gear}} = \frac{30}{10} = \frac{3}{1}$$

Gear ratio is written as 1:3 because it takes 1 turn of the driver to 3 turns of the driven.

Whenever you are asked in an exam how to make something move faster or slower, or with less force or greater force, use the principles explained above.

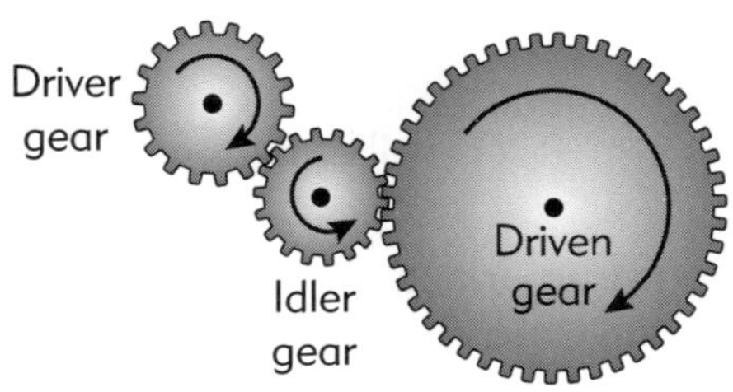

A gear train: driver gear, idler gear and driven gear.

Key words

Gears are wheels with teeth that can be fitted to a shaft.

Gear trains are where one gear wheel is meshed (connected) to another gear wheel in order to make it drive (move).

Gearing down is when the input gear, the 'driver', has fewer teeth than the output gear, the 'driven'.

Gearing up is when the input gear, the 'driver', has more teeth than the output gear, the 'driven'.

- Idler gears are used to change the direction of rotation. Since two gears meshed together will result in them moving in opposite directions, the idler gear ensures that the input and output directions of rotation are the same. Idler gears do not have any effect on the output speed.
- Bevel gears have bevelled (sloping) sides to enable them to drive shafts at 90 degrees to one another.
- Worm and wormwheel gears also change the angle of rotation through 90 degrees. The worm has one tooth and must be the driver gear in order to produce large speed reductions. This type of gearing system is used on electric food mixers where speeds produced by the motor can be reduced.
- Rack and pinion gears change rotary input movement into linear output movement. Rack and pinion gears are used as the steering mechanism on cars and also to open and close the drawer on a CD player.

a) Bevel gear.

b) Worm and wormwheel gears.

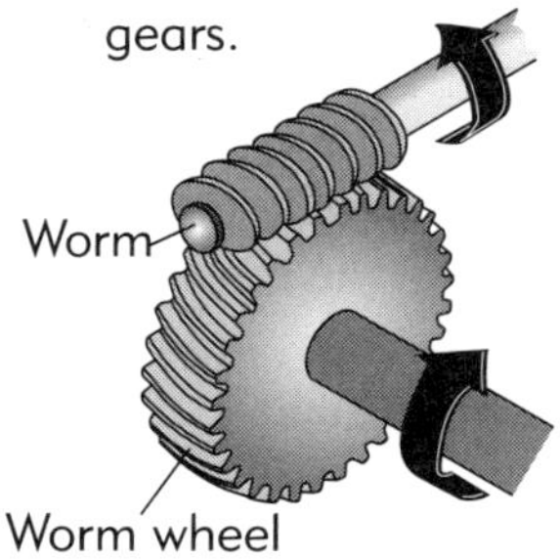

c) Rack and pinion gear.

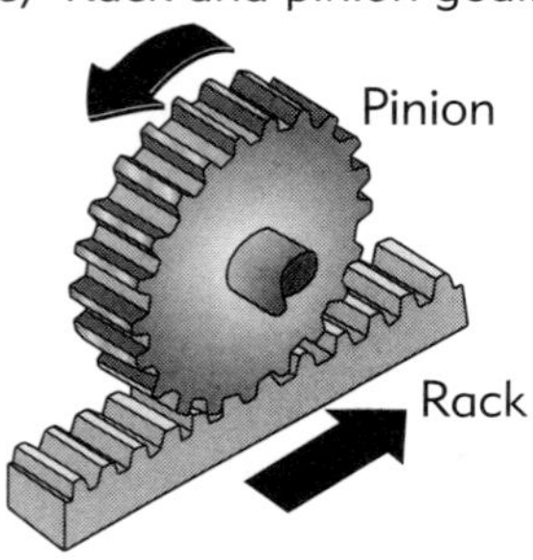

Cams and cranks

Cams are devices for changing rotary input motion into reciprocating output motion. There are many different-shaped cams including eccentric, pear and snail.

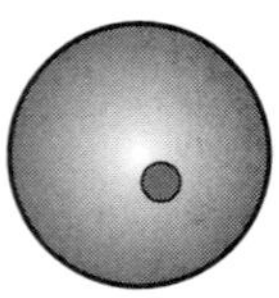

a) Eccentric cam.

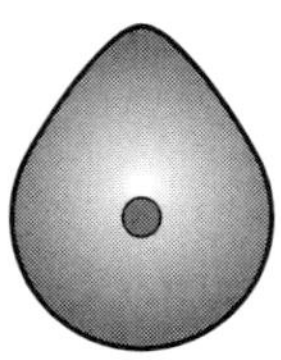

b) Pear cam.

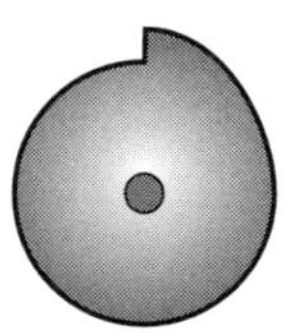

c) Snail cam.

Cams rotate and push a 'follower' up and down according to the shape of the cam. They are used in car engines to open and close valves while children's toys may use them for more amusing purposes such as making a clown's hat move up and down.

Cranks are turning handles that are made longer to achieve greater leverage in order to make turning easier. Examples of a crank are the pedals on a bicycle and the handle on a can opener.

Cranks.

Levers and linkages

Levers are rods that move about a fulcrum or pivot point.

Linkages are formed by joining two or more levers together. The linkages below show the input and output and the directions of movement.

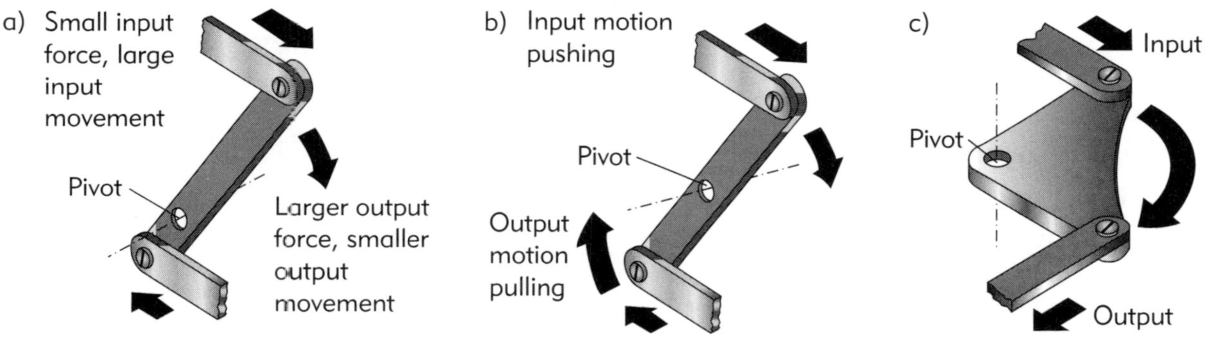

Three examples of linkages.

There are many uses for linkages including pedal bins, bicycle brakes, music stands and umbrellas.

Pulley systems

Pulleys are wheels that are connected by means of belts. Some wheels have grooves in which the belts run. Pulleys are used to transmit movement from one part of a mechanical system to another.

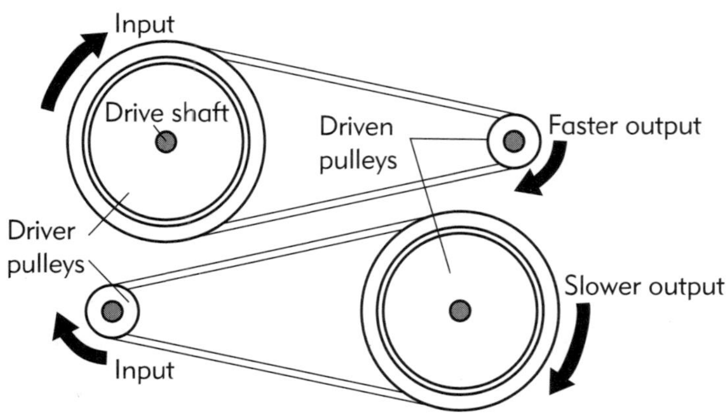

Pulley system.

The pulley system on a drilling machine is an example of how movement is transmitted from the 'driver' pulley (connected to the motor), to the 'driven' pulley (connected to the spindle and chuck).

Pulley systems are used to lift and lower venetian blinds and to transmit the movement from the motor to the brushes of a vacuum cleaner or from the motor to the rotating drum of a washing machine.

Key points

You must be able to:

- explain that a system has three parts
- explain how 'feedback' is used in a system
- explain how sub-systems are used to control production processes
- identify and describe four types of movement: linear, reciprocating, rotary and oscillating
- identify, describe and use mechanisms to bring about required changes and control movement, including: gear systems, cams and cranks, levers and linkages and pulley systems.

Questions

1 Describe the input and output when using a bicycle pump.

2 Explain the difference between 'driver' and 'driven' gear in a gear system.

3 Name four methods of control used when operating a drilling machine.

4 Name the type of output motion made by:

  a a pneumatic drill

  b turning a key in a lock

  c hammering a nail into a piece of wood

  d firing an arrow from a crossbow.

5 What is the purpose of an idler gear?

6 Name a mechanism that is used to change rotary input motion into reciprocating output motion.

Activities

1 **a** Look carefully at the gear system on a bicycle. Count the number of sprockets on the rear wheel and those connected to the pedals.

  b Draw the gear system and draw the position of the chain on the front and rear sprockets when cycling up a steep hill.

2 Consider a toaster as a mechanical and electrical system.

  a Describe the input → process → output when operating the toaster.

  b List as many of the sub-systems as you can and explain how control is built into the system.

3 Examine a double-glazed window that can be opened and closed. Using some card as a base, brass fasteners and card strips as the linkages, make a working model of the linkage mechanism.

4 Select a variety of kitchen appliances that include moving parts. Identify the type of motion made by each part.

Products and applications

This section will cover:

- Establishing the exact function of the product.
- Identifying the parts from which the product is made and how they contribute to the success of the design of the product.
- Establishing how the product works.
- Identifying the materials from which the product is made and the manufacturing processes used to make it.
- Establishing the intended market for the product.
- Comparing and assessing the performance of products with similar function.

This section is tested in the written exam by one question in each of Papers 1, 2, 3 and 4. The questions in Papers 1 and 2 will be based on information provided within the questions, while the questions in Papers 3 and 4 will be based on a common theme published by the exam board and sent to your school.

Imagine that the theme you were required to study was 'Study-chairs'. Breaking down the product analysis into separate areas allows you to study the product more effectively.

Exam questions used to test your knowledge and understanding of the theme always ask, in the last part of the question, to design a modification or improvement to the product.

Establishing the exact function of the product

A swivel chair.

The drawing above shows a chair that could be used for a variety of purposes, including working at a computer at home or in an office. The features of the chair make it a very successfully designed product:

- Armrests for comfort relieve strain on the neck, back and shoulders.
- Feet provide a stable base.
- Castors enable the chair to move smoothly and easily.
- Shaped and padded back for comfort.
- Height adjustable by means of 'gas-lift' system.
- Spring-loaded back to give continual support.
- Shaped and padded seat can swivel through 360 degrees.

Identifying the parts from which the product is made and how they contribute to the success of the design of the product

Many of these chairs are designed for self-assembly and are made up of a number of separate parts, including:

- a base unit with gas-lift system to adjust the seat height
- castors that fit into the ends of the five feet
- a back (padded and upholstered)
- a seat (padded and upholstered)
- armrests
- metal connecting pieces.

The connecting pieces enable the seat, back and armrests to be located and secured. The separate parts can be assembled and secured by means of a screwdriver.

Establishing how the product works

This type of chair provides high levels of comfort while working at a desk.

- Seat height adjustment is achieved by means of a 'gas-lift' system. This works by the user releasing a lever which allows the pressure inside the unit to force the seat upwards. To lower the seat height, the user simply sits on the seat and the weight forces the seat down against the pressure.
- Seat depth can be adjusted forward or back by means of releasing a screw thread connected to a large round handle. The seat can then be slid to the required position and tightened.
- The back can be adjusted up or down using the same principle as for the seat depth.
- The back is spring loaded and is able to tilt forward or back. This means that it can give continual support as well as being locked in one position.
- Castors fitted into each of the five feet enable the chair to be moved smoothly, quickly and easily.

Identifying the materials from which the product is made and the manufacturing processes used to make it

- The seat, back, armrests and base unit feet are made from polypropylene plastic and are injection moulded.
- The metal connecting pieces that also allow for adjustment are made from mild steel and are pressed to the required shape.

Establishing the intended market for the product

This type of chair is produced for two specific markets: the home or domestic market and the industrial or commercial market. Manufacturers produce chairs of different quality and with a range of different features depending on the amount and type of use the chairs will receive.

Home or domestic market

Customers will purchase an individual chair to suit their own specific needs and budget, for example to use in a bedroom or study. Retailers will sell to the public, value-for-money chairs with different features in order to appeal to a wide variety of tastes and needs.

Industrial or commercial market

Customers will purchase chairs in quantity. They are likely to buy chairs with more features to meet the demands of the office environment. These customers will purchase chairs that are made to a higher specification in terms of materials used and the constructions involved. Generally, these are likely to be made to withstand greater wear and tear than in the home or domestic market. Although these chairs may cost more to produce, this may be offset by discounts offered for buying in bulk.

Comparing and assessing the performance of products with similar function

You could be asked to examine two similar products and describe the advantages and disadvantages of them or choose which of the two is the better product.

Consider the two chairs shown below. They both have similar functions as they can be used while working at a desk. Each chair is analysed and assessed for its performance in the table below.

Swivel chair.

Folding chair.

Swivel chair.

Advantages	**Disadvantages**
Adjustable seat height and depth	Relatively expensive
Castors to assist manoeuvrability	Fairly bulky, takes up space
Armrests for support and comfort	
Padded and upholstered	
Colour coordinated	
Well-made, durable materials	

Folding chair.

Advantages	Disadvantages
Lightweight	Will not withstand wear and tear
Folds away to a compact size	One size may not fit all body sizes and shapes
Relatively cheap	No adjustment
Available in sets of four	Cannot be moved across the floor without being lifted

Key points

You must be able to:

- explain the exact function of a product
- identify the separate parts from which a product is made and explain how, together, the parts make a product function successfully
- explain how a product works
- identify the materials from which a product is made and explain the manufacturing processes involved
- identify and explain the intended market for a product
- compare products that have a similar function and identify the strengths and weaknesses of their design.

Questions

1. From the design features listed under 'Establishing the exact function of the product' (see page 79), select four that you would expect as 'standard' on all chairs of this type. Give reasons for your choice.
2. Give four examples where the designer of the adjustable chair has considered anthropometrics (measurements of the human body) in the design of the adjustable chair.
3. Explain why chairs manufactured for industrial use are made to a higher specification.

Activities

Carry out a product analysis of a mobile phone. Ask yourself the following questions:

- What are the main materials used?
- Name the manufacturing process used to produce the plastic body.
- Why is this process suitable for mass production?
- How has the designer considered ergonomics (used by human beings) in the design of the phone?
- Who would buy this product, for example is there a specific market?
- Is colour important to the design of the product?
- How has the manufacturer made sure that the product is of high quality?
- Are there any modifications or improvements that could be made to the design of the phone?

Quality

This section will cover:

- How the quality of products is ensured during manufacture.
- How far products satisfy the needs of customers and how well they fulfil their purpose.
- The importance of accuracy when assembling products.
- The right choice of resources and materials for manufacture and maintenance.
- Social, moral, economic, environmental and aesthetic implications for the design and manufacture of products.

The most important part of this section is for you to be able to understand the difference between the 'quality of design' and the 'quality of manufacture'.

Because much of the information in this section is discussed in more detail elsewhere, it is important that you read the earlier information carefully with 'quality' in mind.

How the quality of products is ensured during manufacture

When you manufactured your product for your internally assessed coursework project you designed a control system to make sure that, when batch produced, each of the products would be of the same high standard. You may have used a jig, former or template to help achieve this 'quality of manufacture'. (See pages 19–22 for information about jigs, formers, and so on.)

When products are manufactured commercially in large quantities 'quality control' is an essential part of the process. Checks are made on samples during and after the manufacturing process. (See pages 34–5 for information about quality control.)

How far products satisfy the needs of customers and how well they fulfil their purpose

It is possible to manufacture a product to a high standard only to find that the product itself is poorly designed. For example, you could manufacture a beautifully crafted children's toy, then find that it creates no interest or excitement for the child. This could be the result of poor or inaccurate initial research.

Another example is the three-wheeled, battery-powered C5 tricycle designed by Sir Clive Sinclair and launched in 1985. The tricycle was intended for use by commuters as an alternative to petrol and diesel-fuelled vehicles in busy city centres. It was an innovative design; clean and efficient, but it was a failure for a variety of reasons. The media criticised the C5 as a 'joke' pointing out that the sitting or lying down position of the user made him or her highly vulnerable next to high-sided vehicles. Although well made, very few were sold.

The importance of accuracy when assembling products

Consider the frame of a small coffee table that is about to be glued together and held in sash cramps. It would be important to carry out two checks to ensure the accuracy and quality of the product:

1 The frame must go together square. To do this, the angle between the leg and rail must be 90 degrees. A try square would be used to check this.

2 The legs must not be 'in winding'. This means making sure that when you look along the edges of the two legs, these edges are parallel.

(See pages 61–3 for information about testing for square and other operations to do with material preparation.)

The right choice of resources and materials for manufacture and maintenance

It is important that the materials chosen for a product are appropriate (suitable) for the way the product will be used. (See pages 44–69 for information about materials, their properties and uses.)

It is also important to consider how maintenance of the product could be carried out. The design of a product must allow for the replacement of parts that may break, rot, rust or wear out. For example, aluminium would be a good choice of material for a ladder since aluminium does not rust and it is strong yet lightweight.

Consider a wooden picnic table that may be left outdoors throughout the year in all weather conditions. In time, the legs may rot from the ends upwards as a result of standing in damp conditions. It would be an advantage if the legs were secured to the rest of the table by means of nuts and bolts rather than a permanent joint such as a glued mortise and tenon joint, to allow for replacement legs to be fitted when needed.

Social, moral, economic, environmental and aesthetic implications for the design and manufacture of products

It is estimated that more than one half of the population owns a mobile phone. The main advantage of the product is that of convenience.

The mobile phone has a variety of excellent design features:

- It is compact so it can be carried easily.
- It is comfortable to handle because it has been ergonomically designed.
- It has a clear visual layout.
- It makes effective use of sound within the design.
- It is aesthetically attractive (looks good).

However, designers have social, moral, economic and environmental responsibilities. Mobile phones are a good example of a product that raises many social, moral, economic, environmental and aesthetic implications:

- Mobile phones cost money. Some people will buy a phone without fully understanding the cost implications of rental contracts or the charges made for calls.

- Some people view the phone as a fashion item and are keen to have the latest model with advanced features.
- What happens to unwanted mobile phones? What provision have manufacturers and retailers made to collect and recycle old phones?
- Recent medical research suggests that prolonged use of mobile phones over a long period of time may cause brain damage. To minimise the risk, manufacturers would need to reposition the phone aerial to the bottom of the phone rather than along the side of the head. To do this would be an admission on the part of the phone companies that their product was, in some way, harmful.

Similar issues are also discussed on page 38.

Key points

You must be able to:

- explain the difference between the quality of design and the quality of manufacture
- explain how quality control can be applied during product manufacture
- explain that some products that are well designed may be poorly manufactured, while products that are badly designed could be manufactured to a high quality
- explain how accuracy can be ensured when assembling products
- ensure that products are manufactured from suitable materials and that maintenance of the product is an important part of the design
- explain how designers and manufacturers have social, moral, environmental and aesthetic responsibilities for their products.

Questions

1 Name three different products where high levels of accuracy of assembly would be important to the function of the product.

2 Explain why the use of permanent joints when constructing products can be a disadvantage to future maintenance.

3 Explain why 'quality control' is built into manufacturing processes.

4 Describe how products such as mobile phones can have social and economic drawbacks.

Activities

1 Carry out a search on the Internet to find out about the Sinclair C5.
   a How many were produced?
   b How much did they cost?
   c What was special about the type of battery used to power the C5?
   d What materials were used for the body?

2 Look around your home and choose a variety of household products. Ask yourself these questions:
   a How well do they work? (quality of design)
   b How well made are they? (quality of manufacture)
   c How suitable are the materials?
   d Has the designer allowed for future maintenance?

Health and safety

This section will cover:

- Designers and consumers.
- Workers involved in the production processes.
- Personal safety.
- Risk assessment.
- Environmental effects.

When new products are designed and manufactured it is important that they are safe to make and safe to use.

Health and safety is concerned with the well-being of everyone involved with the products during their manufacture and with consumers who purchase the products and use them.

Designers and consumers

- Products must be able to withstand misuse, for example a child's toy that falls apart when it is accidentally dropped could be dangerous to the child. Therefore, it is important to consider the choice of materials, construction or manufacturing processes and the finish that is applied.
- Products must conform to safety standards in all countries where they may be sold, for example the lion mark on a child's toy sold in Europe.
- Where necessary, products should include detailed instructions on use, for example when using an electric lawn mower or a food processor.
- Where maintenance of a product may be undertaken by consumers, it must be safe to do so, for example when replacing the blade on an electric lawn mower or cleaning the blades on the food processor.
- Some products may need specific labelling about possible dangers, for example a label on a light bulb giving the safe maximum wattage.

Workers involved in the production processes

You need to consider the working environment in which the products are manufactured and the conditions under which the workers operate:

- The workplace must be well organised so that specific tasks may be carried out safely, for example a heat treatment area such as a welding bay kept separate from other production areas.
- Walkways or gangways should be clearly marked and there should be specific areas where consumable goods or tools are stored out of the way to avoid obstacles.

- Chemicals, solvents, flammable and toxic substances must be stored and handled with extreme care. Employers are required by law to carry out 'risk assessments' of these substances (see below).
- There should be adequate space at workstations so that machine operators can work safely.
- Lighting should be adequate for tasks to be undertaken safely.
- The temperature in which employees work should be comfortable, taking into account the type of processes being undertaken.
- Where machinery is used, it is essential that:
  - instructions for use are clearly displayed near to the machine
  - warning hazards and regulations relating to safety clothing or eye protection are clearly displayed
  - companies provide adequate training in the use of machinery
  - emergency 'stop' buttons are provided
  - regular maintenance is carried out to ensure that tools are safe
  - faulty machinery should be clearly labelled and taken out of use.
- Procedures for emergency evacuation in the event of a fire and the reporting of accidents should be clearly displayed.

a) Wear eye protection.
b) Caution corrosive substance.
c) Smoking and naked flames prohibited.
d) First aid.

Hazard/safety symbols.

Personal safety

Protective wear

- Goggles provide eye protection when using the drilling machine, lathe, sanding disk or certain types of machine saw.
- Face masks or respirators should be used when spray painting and during any operation that creates dust such as sanding.
- Visors give full face protection when casting hot metal.
- Aprons give general protection to clothing while leather aprons are particularly suited to operations such as casting hot metals.
- Leggings should be worn when casting hot metals.
- Rubber/plastic disposable gloves should be worn when using chemicals.
- Steel-capped shoes should be worn where heavy work is undertaken.
- Ear defenders should be used when drilling or cutting with heavy machinery.

Machine guards

Machine guards are designed to protect the operator from a variety of dangers by enclosing the tool behind impact-resistant clear plastic shielding. Some guards such as those around a drilling machine are designed to adjust up and down as the drill bit is brought down onto the workpiece.

With some machines, the danger may be the sharpness of the cutting tool or an abrasive surface which can cause injury.

With many machines, the danger is the moving parts which could cause operators or their clothing to become entangled in the machine.

Some of the machines you may be familiar with must, by law, have adequate guards:

- drill
- lathe
- milling machine.

Dust and fume extraction

Precautions must be taken when carrying out processes that create dust, for example using a sanding disk. Airborne particles can be breathed in or enter the eyes.

Processes that create toxic fumes, such as spray painting or working with glass-reinforced plastic resins, also require great care.

Dust and fume extraction units are very effective when they are fitted closely and directly to the machine or equipment.

Disposal of waste

Within manufacturing environments, there is likely to be waste. It is important that waste materials are not allowed to build up and that they are disposed of properly. Much waste from wood, metal and plastic is relatively harmless, but chemicals need to be disposed of by specialist companies which collect them from the manufacturers' premises.

Barrier creams

Some chemicals such as catalysts and resins used in glass-fibre work can harm the skin and may cause irritation or even a skin disease called dermatitis. To minimise this risk, gloves should be worn. In addition, barrier cream rubbed into the hands and arms will provide a high level of protection. After use, the cream should be washed off with soap and water.

Accident procedures

In the workshop it is essential that you know what to do in the event of an accident.

- Don't panic!
- Always tell the teacher immediately, no matter how minor you may consider the accident to be.
- Know where the first aid box is.
- Know where the emergency stop buttons are in the workshop.

Risk assessment

Risk assessment is the process, required by law, to be undertaken by companies, including schools, to identify potentially dangerous situations in their places of work and to explain how the risks may be reduced or eliminated so that everyone connected with the company can operate in a safe and healthy environment.

There are five stages in carrying out a risk assessment:

1. Identify the process, operation or substance.
2. Identify the possible hazard.
3. Consider the risk, that is, how likely it is that the hazard will occur.
4. Explain the control measures you need to carry out to provide protection.
5. Explain what emergency measures you need to carry out in the event of personal injury.

COSHH

COSHH is the way that employers assess the risks from using substances that could be very dangerous to our health and is one part of risk assessment.

Instructions relating to potentially hazardous substances
There are many potentially dangerous substances used in school workshops including Tensol cement, 'superglue', impact adhesives and some paints. Your teachers will have carried out risk assessments for each of these substances.

Look at the following risk assessment for students and teachers using Tensol cement.

Key word

COSHH stands for the Control of Substances Hazardous to Health.

Risk assessment for Tensol cement.

Process or operation	**Hazards**	**Risk assessment**	**Control measures**
Spreading cement onto surfaces of acrylic plastic to be joined together	**1** May enter through the skin and by swallowing	**1** There would have to be a huge spillage in the workshop or it would have to be used in a very confined space to pose a real hazard.	**1** Use in well-ventilated areas.
	2 Irritant to the skin, eyes and lungs	**2** Splashes from the cement would need to be kept off the skin and away from eyes.	**2** Apply barrier cream and/or wear protective gloves. Eye protection must be worn.
	3 Highly flammable	**3** Vapour from Tensol could be ignited by flames or red-hot metal.	**3** Work must be kept at least 1 m away from flames or red-hot metal.

Instructions relating to the use of portable power tools
The use of portable power tools in schools is becoming more popular. Many students use cordless drills, jig saws and power routers. Manufacturers of portable power tools must, by law, provide adequate instructions relating to their use. It is essential that the instructions are read carefully and then put into practice when the tools are used.

Environmental effects

For information on the effects of pollution and waste disposal, see pages 69–70.

Key points

You must be able to:

- explain the ways in which designers and manufacturers must ensure that products are safe to use
- explain ways by which the working environment meets health and safety regulations
- explain how personal safety is protected in the manufacturing environment
- carry out risk assessments for substances and processes
- understand the problems, in terms of health and safety, that waste disposal creates for the environment.

Questions

1 Explain three ways in which designers and manufacturers can ensure that a product is safe to use.
2 List four features you would expect to find in a well-organised and 'safe' workshop.
3 State two reasons why it is necessary to have safety guards fitted to a drilling machine or centre lathe.
4 Describe two safety precautions you would take when spray painting.
5 Explain the difference between a 'hazard' and a 'risk'.

Activities

1 Make a room plan of one of your school workshops.
  a Draw onto the plan the positions of the workbenches, tables, cupboards, machines, emergency stop buttons, and so on.
  b Make a list of all the 'good' or safe features and a list of all the 'poor' or potentially unsafe features.
2 Carry out two risk assessments. The first should be for a process such as using a drilling machine or a scroll saw; the other should be when using a substance such as a polyurethane varnish or impact adhesive.

Specimen exam questions

Question 1

Figure 1 shows some details of a small table on which drinks and snacks could be placed.
The table top can be adjusted to different heights.
The table top has been lifted off to show details of the frame to which it will be attached.

Figure 1.

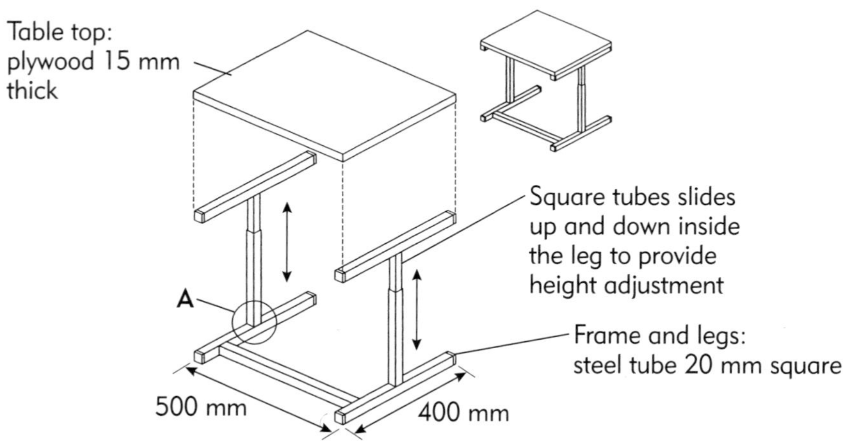

(a) Name a permanent method of joining the steel tube at **A**.

Brazing ✓ (1)

(b) Name the abrasive method you would use to clean-up the steel frame.

emery cloth ✓ (1)

(c) State a suitable finish for:

(i) the table top

Varnish ✓ (1)

(ii) the steel frame

plastic coating (dip coat) ✓ (1)

(d) The table top is to be connected to the frame by a method that allows it to be removed for maintenance.
Use a sketch and notes to show a suitable method. (2)

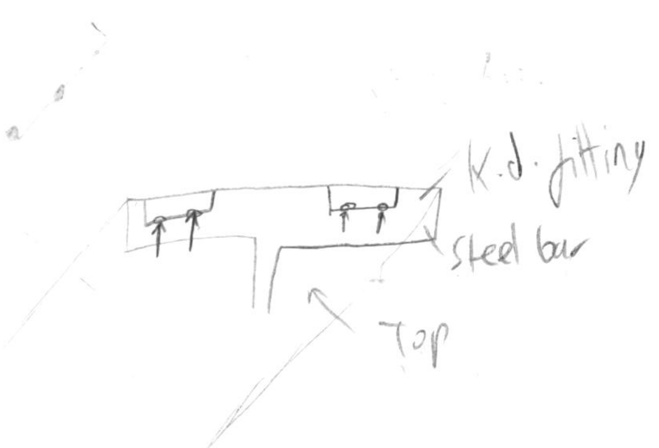

Question 2

Figure 2 shows views of a free-standing clock.
The clock is made from two separate pieces of acrylic plastic.

Figure 2.

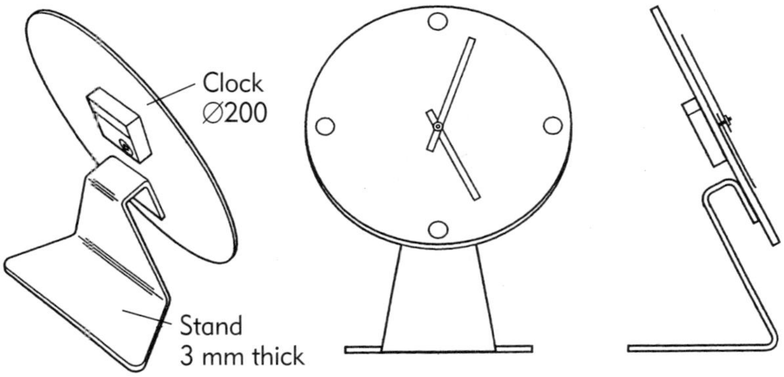

(a) State **one** reason why a designer would construct a mock-up model of the clock before making it from acrylic plastic.

Can see if product is what they want (check appearance) ✓ (1)

Figure 3 shows the development (net) of the stand marked out on a sheet of acrylic plastic.

Figure 3.

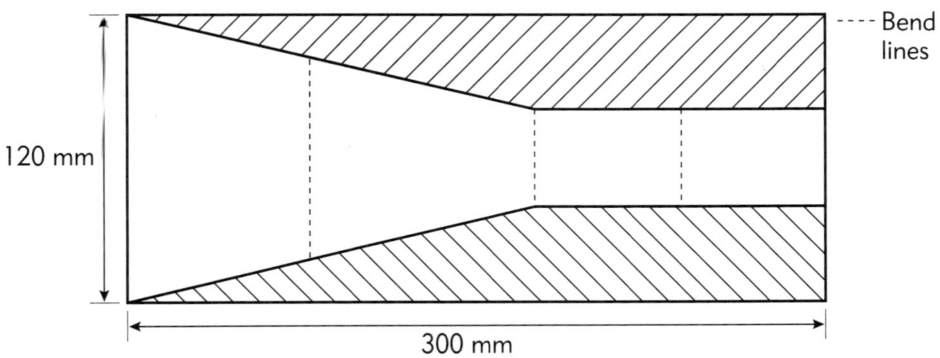

(b) The table below gives some of the stages in making the clock stand.
Complete the table.

Stage	Description of process	Tools/equipment
1	Mark out acrylic	felt tip
2	Cut outline shape	Jig saw
3	Clean + smooth edges	file
4	Bend acrylic to shape	bending jig

(6)

(c) Explain how a computer could be used to help in **either** the design **or** the manufacture of the clock.

CAD could used to make models etc of the clock stand, from this the manufacturer can look at sizes shape etc, the process in general (2)

Question 3

Figure 4 shows a design for a Compact Disc (CD) rack made from acrylic plastic.

Figure 4.

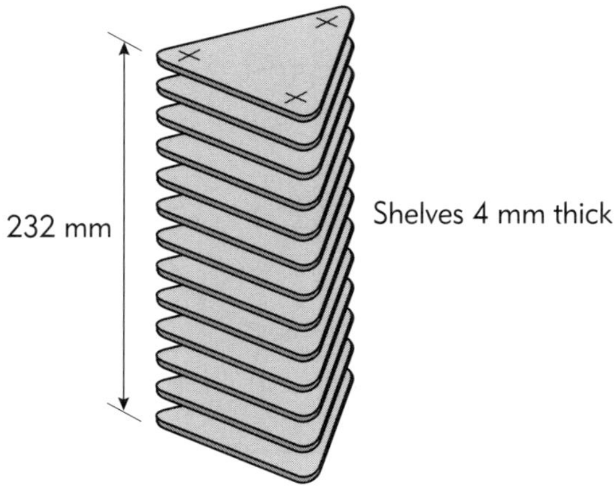

(a) Use notes and sketches to show how each shelf could be spaced to enable CDs to be stored. (3)

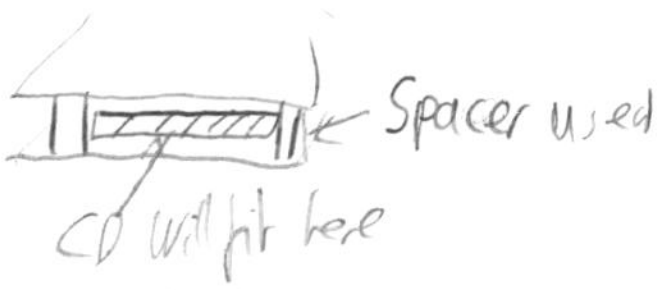

(b) Explain **two** ways in which the designer had considered ergonomics in the design of the CD rack.

1 Position for holes .... (1)

2 Secure while drilling .... (1)

Figure 5 shows one shelf of the CD rack.

Figure 5.

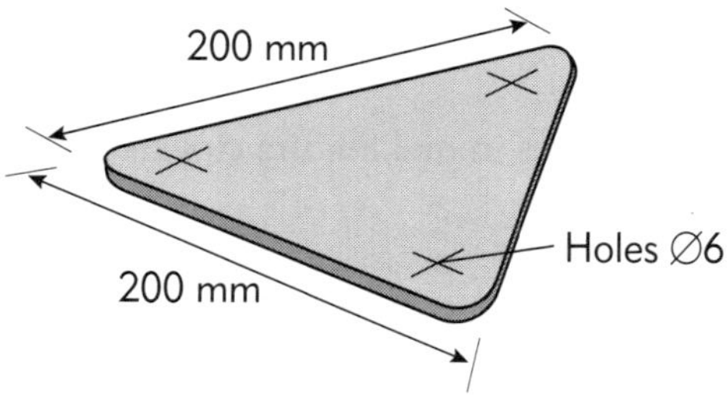

(c) **(i)** Use notes and sketches to design a jig that could be used when drilling the **three** holes in each of the twelve shelves accurately. (3)

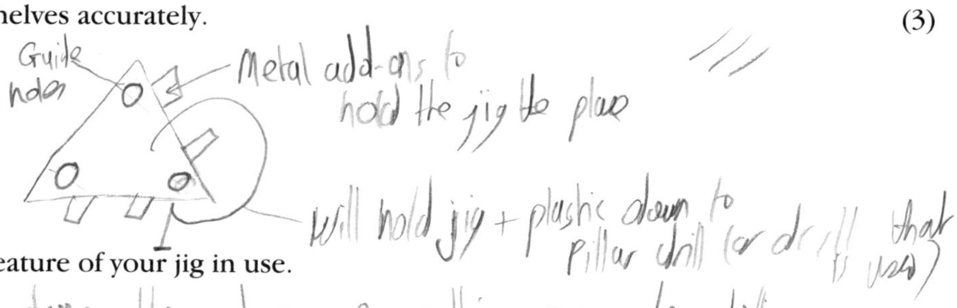

(ii) Explain **one** safety feature of your jig in use.

The G-clamp - this keeps everything secure when drilling .... (1)

Question 4

Figure 6 shows two views of a child's toy.
When the tail is pushed or pulled, the legs and head are made to move in the directions shown.

Figure 6.

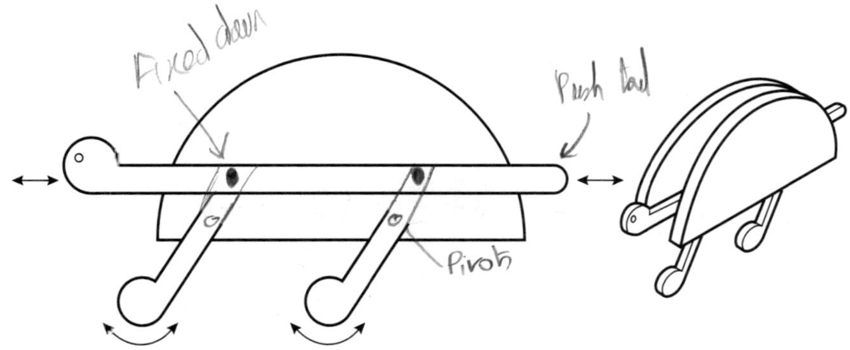

Front panel removed
to show incomplete mechanism.

(a) Name the type of motion made by:

(i) the head.. (1)

(ii) the legs .... (1)

(b) On the incomplete view above, draw a suitable mechanism that would move the head and legs as shown.
Label the parts of the mechanism. (5)

Figure 7 shows a view of a similar toy with an incomplete mechanism.
When the tail is pushed, the legs move in opposite directions as shown by the arrows.

Figure 7.

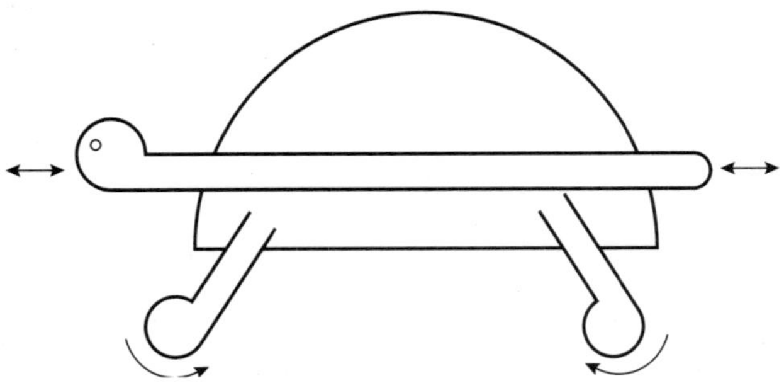

(c) Complete Figure 7 to show a suitable mechanism that would move the legs as shown. (3)

(d) Add to Figure 7 a method of limiting the distance moved by the head. (2)

Question 5

Figure 8 shows details of a cubed puzzle game. By moving the puzzle, the marble is to be located in the centre of the base.

Figure 8.

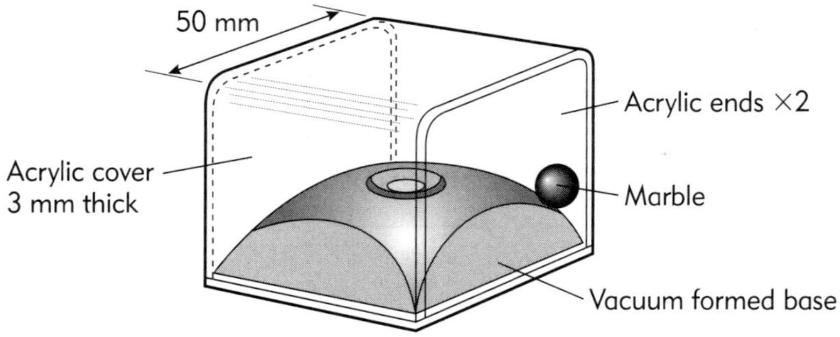

(a) Sketch a bending jig that will allow the acrylic cover to be bent into the shape shown. (3)

(b) The base of the game is to be vacuum formed.

(i) Name a suitable material for the base other than acrylic.

.... (1)

(ii) Figure 9 shows an incomplete section through a vacuum forming machine. Complete Figure 9 to show the machine set up for forming the base of the game.

Figure 9. (3)

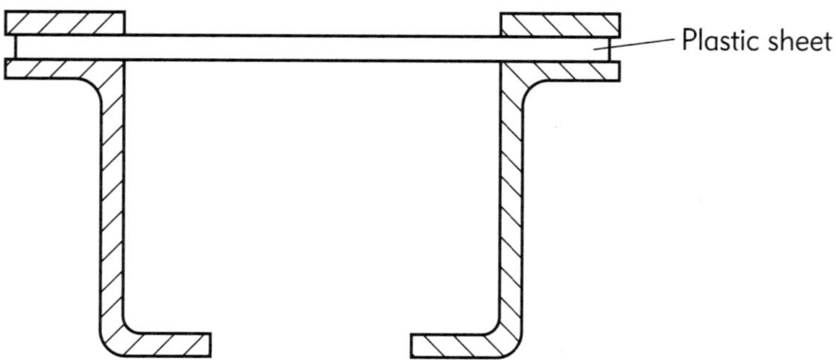

Question 6

This question is based on the theme 'hand-held mechanical kitchen appliances'.
Figure 10 shows two different gear systems used in hand-held mixers/beaters.

Figure 10.

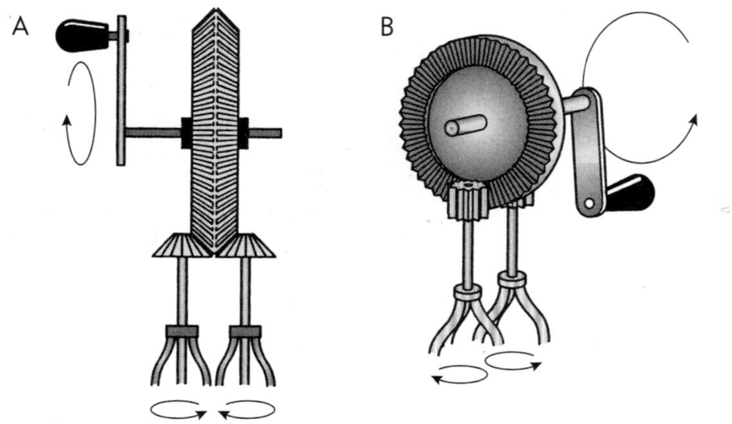

(a) Name two different gear systems shown in Figure 10.

1 .... (1)

2 .... (1)

(b) Gear wheels for the mixers can be made from metal or plastics.

(i) Describe **two** advantages of using gear wheels made from plastics.

1 .... (1)

2 .... (1)

(ii) Name a suitable plastic for making gear wheels.

.... (1)

(iii) Name a process used to manufacture plastic gear wheels.

.... (1)

(c) When buying a hand-operated mixer, describe **two** features that would influence your choice.

Feature 1 ....

....

.... (2)

Feature 2 ....

....

.... (2)

Question 7

Figure 11 shows a video cassette storage unit made mainly from a good quality hardwood. The video cassettes are shown in position.

Figure 11.

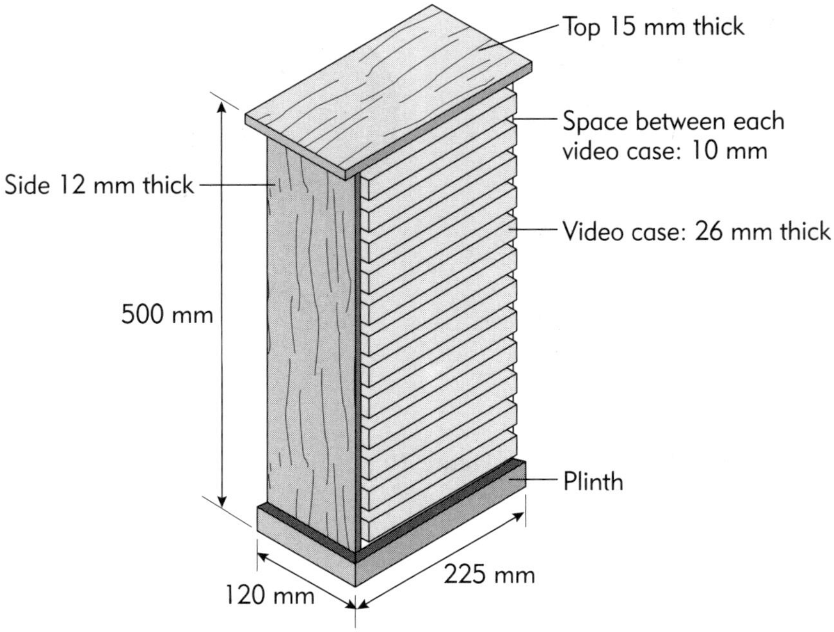

(a) State **two** ways in which the designer had considered ergonomics in the design of the video storage unit.

1 .... (1)

2 .... (1)

(b) (i) State **one** visual characteristic of hardwood that gives it a quality appearance.

.... (1)

(ii) Name an appropriate finish other than varnish that would enhance the appearance of the hardwood video unit.

.... (1)

Figure 12 shows part-views of the top and sides of the unit.

Figure 12.

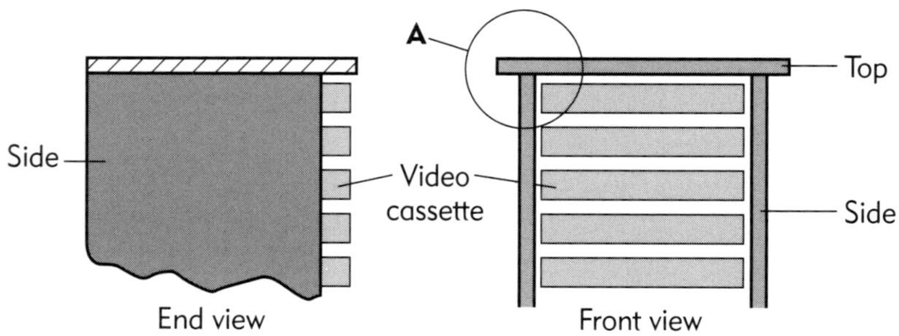

(c) Sketch and name a suitable construction to join the top and sides at **A** in Figure 12. (2)

Named construction .... (1)

(d) A plinth could be made from four separate pieces of hardwood joined at the corners by means of a glued mitre joint.
Add notes and sketches to the plan view of the plinth below, to describe a suitable method of securely holding the mitre joints together while the glue sets. (2)

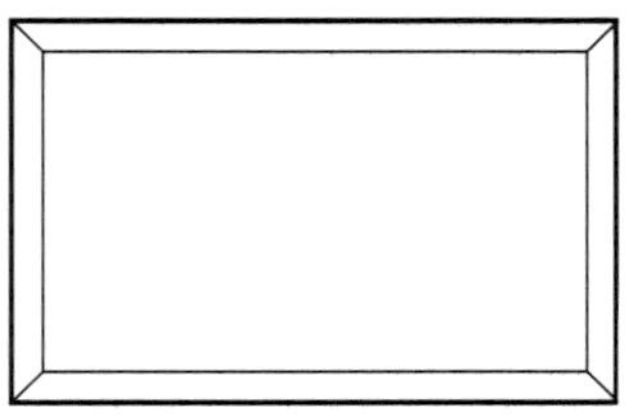

Answers to questions

Part 1 Designing and Making

Developing and writing a design brief/Drawing up a specification (page 12)

1
- Where would the rack be located?
- What types of magazines/journals do you have?
- What sizes are the magazines?
- How many magazines do you want to store?

2 Any two of the following:
- What equipment do you want the desk tidy to store?
- What sizes are the items to be stored?
- How many items are to be stored?

3 Environmental issues, monetary costs, available resources.

Generating design proposals (page 17)

1 Any two of the following modifications:
- Different shaped base with more shapes.
- Different shapes including, for example, a rectangle and hexagon.
- Use of bright colours to attract young children.
- Use of numbers, letters or pictures on the shapes.

2 Advantages of making the toy from two separate pieces: you can drill straight through the top piece and glue it to the bottom piece rather than have to work to the required depth; much quicker and neater.

3 Functional requirements of the mirror – any two of the following:
- Must be adjusted and locked at any angle between 0 and 45 degrees.
- Must be easy to adjust and lock.
- Must not damage the surface on which it is positioned.

Product development (page 23)

1 Speed up production and reduce manufacturing costs; ensure repetitive accuracy.

2 To assist sawing, drilling, bending and shaping.

3 Any three of the following design features:
- The workpiece is held securely in place during the operation.
- Simple and straightforward to use.
- Quick and easy to adjust (if required).
- Identical outcomes time and time again.
- Well made and durable to withstand repetitive use.

4 Moulding a toboggan involves heating and injecting plastic granules into a mould to produce a single-piece design. Fabricating a toboggan involves joining separate pieces of hardwood together by means of joints such as screws and glue.

5 Any four of the following reasons for carrying out testing before manufacture:

- To find out how strong the overall structure of the product is.
- To find out which materials are the most suitable.
- To find out the best joints.
- To find out how long it takes to manufacture.
- To find out what the product looks like.
- To find out which components are the most suitable.

Product planning (page 27)

1 **a** There is no thickness of material indicated on the drawing so you will have to suggest an appropriate thickness, for example 15 mm. You will also need to choose a suitable material, for example mahogany.

Cutting list example:

Part name	Number required	Size (mm) (length × width × thickness)	Material
Upright ends	2	135 × 90 × 15	Mahogany
Base	1	240 × 90 × 15	Mahogany

b ***Arrangements of parts to be cut out.***

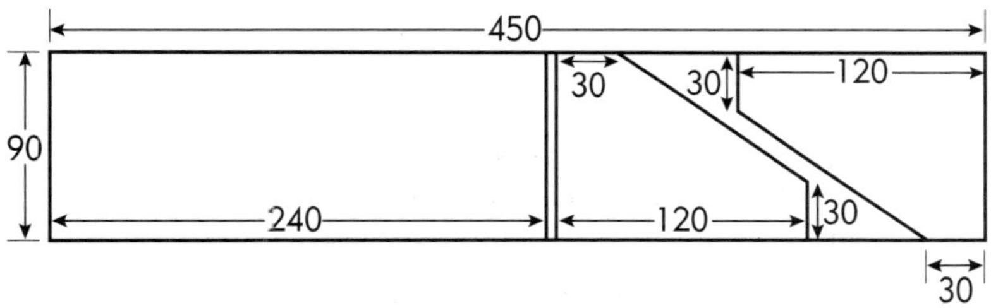

2 Before working out the stages you will need to think about the constructions you would use to join the various parts of the rack, for example you could use a dowel joint for the back rail into the ends and housing joints for the shelves into the ends and the upright partition into the top and bottom shelves.

Five main stages:

i Mark out the dowel and housing joints.
ii Drill and cut out the joints.
iii Assemble dry to test the fit of the joints. Modify if necessary.
iv Glasspaper all inside surfaces that would be difficult to clean up after gluing.
v Glue together with sash cramps.

ICT applications (page 32)

1 Four features of CAD software:

- On-screen modelling allows the product to be rotated and viewed from different angles.
- The product can be made to look as though it is made from different materials.
- Products can be shown from different camera angles and background lighting.
- Products can be made to move on screen to see how they work.

2 When a CNC machine is used to manufacture a product it works from a drawing. The drawings produced by computer are made up of numerical data. This data is processed and converted into data that the machine understands.

3 Rapid Prototyping is a quick means of producing a 3D model of a product that can be tested and evaluated. Saves companies money because design faults can be ironed out prior to full-scale production.

4 Any two of the following advantages of using robots:
- Ability to do boring, repetitive jobs normally undertaken by people.
- Ability to perform tasks in dangerous or hazardous situations.
- Relied upon for high levels of repetitive accuracy.
- Ability to be reprogrammed quickly to switch from one task to another.

5 Any three of the following tool settings:
- Set the correct tool diameter for the tool being used.
- Final depth of cut.
- Maximum depth of cut per pass.
- The clearance of the tool as it passes over the surface of the workpiece.
- The speed of cut along the X-Y axes: horizontal speed across the workpiece.
- The speed of cut in the Z axis: the speed of the tool as it cuts vertically into the surface of the workpiece.

Industrial applications (page 36)

1
- TV sets: repetitive flow mass production. Large quantities of identical products can be made. The system is known as 'in-line' assembly as components are added one at a time along a conveyor belt.
- Plate glass: continual flow production. Raw materials are processed to make the glass and the factory may stay open 24 hours a day all year round as it is too expensive to switch the machinery on and off.
- Pottery mugs: batch production methods, where only a limited number, for example 10–1000 products are required.
- A pair of hand-made earrings: one-off production, as this could be a special order from a customer.

2 People will pay for quality one-off products because of the care and high level of skill that goes into this method of production. Each product is unique. Costs are high because it can be labour intensive and time-consuming.

3 Disadvantage of the just-in-time system: if the delivery of materials, components, and so on, is held up for any reason, then production is halted and this costs companies a great deal of money. Some companies only hold enough materials to maintain production for one hour at a time.

4 Any three of the following reasons why companies build quality assurance and control into their manufacturing systems:
- To reduce production costs by reducing waste and lost time.
- To improve the company's efficiency by making fewer faulty goods.
- To increase company profits.
- To improve a company's reputation.

Product evaluation (page 41)

1 A detailed specification gives a list of requirements that the designer will want a product to meet. It may include details about the market or users, materials and so on. When the product has been made the specification enables the designer to check how well the product works by comparing the performance of the product against each of the points in your specification. The more detailed the specification, the greater the amount of feedback received about the product.

2 Designers and manufacturers can help the environment in any three of the following ways:

- Designing energy efficient products.
- Designing products that last a long time rather than for fashion.
- More efficient production methods to reduce the amount of waste.
- Using materials that can be recycled.
- Reducing unnecessary packaging.
- Using wood from sustained forests.

3 Two advantages of using sheet metal for the bookend:

- It is quicker to manufacture since pieces of wood would need to be fabricated, that is, joined together.
- Because the process is quicker, it would also be more economical if batch or mass produced.

4 **a** To find out how well the products perform in order to determine whether or not they can be improved. Tests would be carried out to find out whether or not the materials, constructions and manufacturing processes are suitable. Tests should be carried out, as far as possible, under identical conditions to those in which the product will operate. Therefore, some tests may need to be carried out over a period of weeks or months.

b To manage the way in which a series of components, operations or activities that, when joined together, enable a specific task to be carried out.

Part 2 Knowledge and Understanding

Materials and pre-manufactured standard components (page 71)

1 **a** Aluminium

b Because of its lightness and strength.

2 To make the metal softer so that it can be formed more easily.

3 Extremely durable; because it contains its own natural oil, it is resistant to moisture, acids and alkalis.

4 Any two of the following advantages of using manufactured boards:

- Much more stable and less likely to twist or warp because of the way they are constructed.
- Available in larger sheet sizes than solid woods.
- More readily available at do-it-yourself stores than solid woods.
- Less expensive.

5 **a** Corner joint on a cabinet.

b To join the rails to the legs of a coffee table.

c Used where a shelf is joined to the side of a cabinet or where a partition is to be inserted in a box or cabinet.

6 Any two of the following reasons for applying a finish to wood or metal:

- to improve the appearance
- to keep the surface clean
- to preserve and protect.

7 Any two of the following: guttering, drainpipes, window profiles, curtain rails.

8 Smart memory alloy (Nitinol) and 'polymorph'. Nitinol is 'intelligent' because SMA works by 'remembering' a shape heated to a specific temperature. At room temperature the SMA wire can be reshaped but when reheated to the original temperature, known as the 'transition temperature', the wire will return to its original shape. Polymorph granules become soft when immersed in hot water. The plastic may then be moulded by hand to the required shape. Polymorph can be considered 'intelligent' because when it is re-immersed in hot water it can be remoulded. At room temperature polymorph can be machined and cut in the same way as other plastics.

9 Any two of the following advantages of recycling:

- Saves non-renewable resources.
- Reduces energy use and gas emissions that damage the atmosphere.
- Helps to control pollution resulting from the manufacturing and disposal processes.
- Reduces the dependence on raw materials.

Systems and control (page 78)

1 Input: pushing and pulling the handle in and out.
Output: the air being forced out of the pump.

2 The driver gear is the gear that provides the movement, for example the gear that is connected directly to an electric motor.
The driven gear is the gear that moves only while it is connected to the driver gear. The driven gear cannot move without this connection.

3 Four methods of control when using a drilling machine include:

- applying the appropriate amount of pressure to drill the material
- a pulley system used to alter the speed
- a drill table set at correct height
- a depth gauge.

4 **a** Reciprocating.
b Rotary.
c Oscillating.
d Linear.

5 An idler gear is positioned between two spur gears to ensure that the two spur gears rotate in the same direction.

6 A cam.

Products and applications (page 82)

1 Any of four of the following features, with reasons:

- Armrests for support, relieving strain on the neck, back and shoulders. Reason: comfort of the operator.
- Feet provide a stable base. Reason: essential that the chair does not topple over.
- Castors enable the chair to move smoothly and easily. Reason: it is important that the operator is able to move across the floor on the chair without having to get off it and walk across, thus saving time.
- Shaped and padded chair back: Reason: comfort of the operator.
- Height adjustable by means of 'gas-lift' system. Reasons: important for the manufacturers to produce a chair that will suit a wide range of body types and sizes and for consumers who will want a chair that meets their individual needs.
- Spring-loaded chair back. Reasons: important that the operator's back is well-supported; a spring-loaded chair back gives continuous support without the operator having to be aware of the need for support.
- Shaped and padded seat can swivel through 360 degrees. Reasons: comfort of the operator; manoeuvrability of the seat makes it convenient and efficient to use.

2 Any four of the following examples of the use of anthropometric data:

- Adjustable seat height – involves measuring the seated height of a person.
- Depth of seat from front to back – involves measuring the distance from the back of the legs to the buttocks.
- Armrests giving support – involves measuring the distance from the shoulder to the elbow.
- Shaped and padded seat – involves measuring the distance across the hips.
- Shaped and padded back – involves measuring the distance across and the height of the back.

3 Because they will be used by more people with different seating 'habits'; they will need to withstand more concentrated use over a period of time.

Quality (page 85)

1 Any three from a wide range of electrical and electronic products, for example TVs, cameras, mobile phones, portable drills, food mixers, computers and larger products including motor cars.

2 Permanent joints can be a disadvantage to some products if, when carrying out regular maintenance, it is not possible to remove parts that need to be. For example, when changing the belt on a vacuum cleaner, it is essential that the connecting parts can be removed easily using a variety of clips, springs and/or screws and nuts and bolts.

3 To ensure that high levels of manufacture are maintained. Quality control is carried out during the manufacturing process as well as at the end. Sampling occurs during manufacture to check, for example, on the consistency of materials used and the tolerances applied to the fit or to finished sizes. To carry out only final quality control checks at the end of manufacture could result in huge financial losses if something has gone wrong during a production run.

4 Economic and social drawbacks of mobile phones:

- Could be considered as expensive 'toys' which, after the initial purchase cost, require the user to pay rental or call charges. Fashion can influence some people who may not fully understand the financial implications of owning a mobile phone.
- Recent medical research suggests a possible link between prolonged use of mobile phones and brain damage.
- What happens to unwanted mobile phones? What provision do retailers and manufacturers make to collect and recycle old phones?

Health and safety (page 90)

1 Any three of the following ways in which designers and manufacturers ensure a product is safe to use:

- Making sure that the materials from which the product is made and the ways by which it is constructed are sound and will withstand some misuse.
- Making sure that products conform to safety standards within those countries where the product will be used.
- Where appropriate, detailed and clear instructions on use and maintenance must be provided.
- Where appropriate, include labelling about possible dangers, limitations to use and so on.

2 Any four of the following:

- Separate designated areas where specific tasks are to be carried out.
- Space in the workshop to walk safely without obstruction from stools or bags.
- Safe storage and racking of all hand tools.
- Safe storage of any potentially dangerous substances.
- Good levels of lighting and appropriate heating/ventilation.
- Well-maintained tools, machines and equipment.
- Adequate instructions/health and safety rules displayed close to machinery.
- Emergency stop buttons easily recognised and accessible.
- Procedures for evacuation and how to deal with emergencies clearly displayed.

3 To protect the machine operator from: the moving/rotating drill or chuck; the danger of material flying from the workpiece when drilling or carrying out lathe turning.

4 Spray in well-ventilated area; wear a face mask.

5 A hazard describes a potential danger, for example that you could burn yourself when using a brazing torch.
A risk describes the likelihood of the hazard actually occurring.

Answers to exam questions

Question 1 (page 92)

(a) Any one of the following: brazing, welding, soldering, plate/bracket and rivet.
(b) Any one of the following: emery cloth, wet or dry, silicon carbide, wire wool.
(c) **(i)** Any one of the following: paint, varnish, polish, wood stain.
(ii) Any one of the following: paint, plating, dip-coat
(d) Suitable method must allow for removal of top.
If nuts and bolts or screws are shown through top (1 mark maximum).
Correct use of screws, nuts and bolts inset or a KD fitting with a sketch showing steel tube and top (2 marks).
Notes relating to method (1 mark).

Question 2 (page 93)

(a) Any one of the following: size, balance, appearance, bends, to show potential customers.

(b)

Stage	Description of process	Tools/equipment	Mark
1	[Mark out acrylic]	Scriber, chinagraph pencil, felt tip, ruler, square, template	1
2	Cut outline shape	Variety of saws including coping, vibro, jig, band (must be fine-toothed, narrow blade)	1/1
3	Clean and smooth edges	Any from: scraper, file, wet or dry paper, polishing mop	1/1
4	[Bend acrylic to shape]	Strip heater, line bender, bending jig, former	1

(c) CAD used to design the 'face' of the clock (1 mark).
Easy to modify, save and print out exact design, virtual view, check size, colour, etc. (1 mark)
Or
CAM used to engrave the surface of the clock face or to cut out numbers, etc. (1 mark)
Accuracy ensured, quality product (1 mark).

Question 3 (page 94)

(a) Use of 'spacer' or similar technique (1 mark).
Quality or crudity of spacer (1 mark).
Added notes/communication (1 mark).

(b) Any two of the following: ease of access, rounded plastic shape, visible access to CDs.

(c) **(i)** Locate jig to shelf (1 mark).
Position for holes located/drilled (1 mark).
Secure while drilling (1 mark).

(ii) Examples of safety features include: plastic held securely, jig operates without fingers too close to drill bit.

Question 4 (page 95)

(a) **(i)** Reciprocating.

(ii) Oscillating.

(b) Guides support for tail and head (1 mark).
Successful movement (1 mark).
Pivots (1 mark).
Detail/accuracy (0–2 marks).
Rack and pinion system accepted.

(c) Complete view: legs extended (1 mark).
Moving pivots identified (1 mark).
Fixed pivots identified (1 mark).
Or: Rack and pinion system accepted (0–3 marks, dependent upon accuracy and clarity).

(d) Movement limited by means of horizontal slots or 'stops' (0–2 marks dependent upon appropriateness of position).

Question 5 (page 96)

(a) Sketch to include location for one end (1 mark), jig (1 mark), holding (1 mark).

(b) **(i)** Any suitable thermoplastic material (not acrylic), e.g. polystyrene, polythene, PVC, ABS, polycarbonate.

(ii) Any three of the following: location of heater, mould shown, table, air evacuation.

Question 6 (page 97)

(a) A: bevel.
B: either of the following: crown and pinion, rack and pinion.

(b) **(i)** Any two of the following: quieter, less lubrication, lighter, will not rot, easier to change, etc.

(ii) Nylon or ABS.

(iii) Injection moulding or compression moulding.

(c) Accept answers that compare the advantages of one mixer with those of the other (2 marks for each qualified answer, 1 mark for one-word unqualified answers x 2). Any two of the following: strength of device or materials (comparative); ease of working or operation; grip or handle being comfortable or holdable; ease of storage unit; ease of taking blades out for cleaning; suitable for use by left-handed people (2 marks).
[Note: hand-operated mixers could be electrical, so look for such mixers having pre-set speeds, easier to eject blades, types of other blades provided, etc. Cost is not accepted as a feature.]

Question 7 (pages 98–9)

(a) Two ergonomic considerations: ease of access – pull out or replace video; clear identification of video – sight.

(b) **(i)** Visual characteristic of hardwood: distinctive, colour and grain.

(ii) Any one of the following: French polish, white polite, wax, teak oil, lacquer and sanding sealer.

(c) Accuracy and quality of sketch (up to 2 marks).
Suitable joint at 'A' named; housing, dowel.

(d) Sketch showing mitre cramps or string cramp (1 mark).
Added notes to explain method (1 mark).